CW00867587

Sammy I Love you

Sammy I Love you

A TRUE STORY OF LOVE AND HOPE

Sally Nielsen

ALLEN&UNWIN
SYDNEY·MELBOURNE·AUCKLAND·LONDON

Published by Allen & Unwin in 2012

Allen & Unwin
Sydney, Melbourne, Auckland, London

83 Alexander Street
Crows Nest NSW 2065
Australia
Phone: (61 2) 8425 0100
Fax: (61 2) 9906 2218
Email: info@allenandunwin.com
Web: www.allenandunwin.com

Cataloguing-in-Publication details are available
from the National Library of Australia
www.trove.nla.gov.au

ISBN 978 1 74237 974 6

Cover photographs from iStockphoto and Shutterstock
Text design by Nada Backovic
Set in 11 / 16 Birka by Bookhouse, Sydney
Printed and bound in Australia by Griffin Press

10 9 8 7 6 5 4 3 2 1

MIX
Paper from
responsible sources
FSC® C009448
www.fsc.org

The paper in this book is FSC® certified.
FSC® promotes environmentally responsible, socially beneficial and economically viable management of the world's forests.

Contents

♥

Author's Note

♥

Dedicated with love to my soulmate Sam, who described our love in this poem:

The most beautiful thing in life
is when two people truly connect
one to say I Love You
two to say it with respect
It's not an idea you flirt with
it comes from deep within
every time I look into your eyes
it smacks me on the chin
Sal, you are incredible
you knock me off my feet

I never thought it could happen so fast
but you are just so sweet
Everything about you
is so incredibly sweet to me
from the way you laugh so sweetly
to the way you look at me
It's a feeling I get when I'm with you
to love when I've never loved before
I feel so incredibly lucky to
have found that one girl I truly adore
It hurts so much to leave you
when things are going so great
but one thing I know for sure is
we were brought together by fate
A shooting star once told me
like an angel from above
that the girl lying next to me
was a girl I could truly love
I write this little poem
to really let you know
that even though I'm going away
our love can only grow
The only way to end this poem
is to once again let you know
I love you, I love you, I love you
more than I could ever show
love, Sammy

(written by Sam in June 2006, as a farewell gift upon his
departure on his three-month overseas working holiday)

Sam, you have given me a gift so powerful only the lucky
ones behold it: love.

I love you,

Sal xxx

Acknowledgements

♥

Without the incredible support of 'Sam's Army' we would not be here together:

The Goddards: John, Leslie, Josh, Luke, Viviana, Myles, Klara and our darling Leila. Your continued support has allowed us to grow together once again, to fight this journey as one.

The Nielsens and Blakeys: Dad, Mum, Amanda, Jono, Jake and Alyce. You always made me feel unconditionally loved and at home, even in the darkest of hours. Your guidance has lit the path I have walked down, and brought me peace and serenity. I love you all.

Louisa, Symone, Michelle and Lisa: you have always listened and provided a place of solace for me. Each of you have kept my feet on the ground, my mind clear, and from some of you, a very necessary stiff beverage in my hand!

The Hillstone Girls, Hans and Jens: you never once pushed me for answers, and you always allowed me an environment where I wasn't 'the girl whose fiancé had a stroke' . . . so thank you.

Ritchie and Kate: your dedication to 'your mate' is astounding and we have always appreciated the support. You kept me on my feet.

Sam's 'boys': you know who you are and what you have done to support us and accommodate our needs. Sam will never forget the love you have all shown him.

Selwa, for giving me new opportunities in life, showing me that a light does always shine and for looking out for me—thank you.

Kate Morton: thank you for introducing our story on *Australian Story*. Without that connection, and your wonderful influence, this book would never have been published.

All the medical staff who worked so hard to keep my Sammy alive, you have the hardest jobs, and you'll never realise how incredibly integral you have all been to our journey.

The rehab team—thank you for being so patient and continually pushing Sam to the next level.

To the carers—Dylan, James and Jesse—what a tough job, but you always keep Sammy smiling and well looked after.

And finally my darling Sam, the light of my life. You are my sunshine, my only sunshine, you make me happy, when skies are grey (and blue).

Life in the Fast Lane

♥

Life was good. In fact, life was great. It was the end of summer, and the days were warm and clear. As the sun set over the back deck of our brand new home, I glanced over at Sam playing with our two dogs, and thought just how lucky we were.

Sam and I had met in the winter of 2004 while I was in my first year of Business Management at the Queensland University of Technology. This particular day, I was crossing the middle of the university grounds with my friend Mark, and we happened to run into his twin brother, Luke, who was walking in our direction with a tall, handsome, vibrant guy. He lit up the space instantly. He was gorgeous, sweet, and had a smile that said 'I am trouble, but you will let me get away with anything.' In a particularly cheeky voice, he introduced himself as Sam Goddard, and gave me a once over. I knew he liked what he saw and I felt an instant attraction. A rush of excitement ran through me. The boys chatted about Sam's upcoming eighteenth birthday party, as I drifted in and out of conversation, thinking about this handsome man.

Before I knew it the conversation was over and we were walking in separate directions, each with one half of the 'Evan's Twins'. To this day I still remember looking back and seeing him look back at me, that cheeky smile wrapped around his face.

The months went by and I was busy with work and uni. A few friends of mine from school invited me to an eighteenth and I agreed to go. As we pulled up to the long grass driveway of the house, the car got stuck in mud and so did our heels as we jumped out of the car with excitement. I don't entirely remember the party, except that it was Sam's, and I saw him doing exactly what he does best—be the life of the party. It was another brief encounter.

The seasons passed and I don't recall seeing Sam again, until two years later. I had spent three months travelling overseas, to London, Paris, Germany, Vienna, Prague and many other beautiful places. I had only been back a short time when the long-term relationship I was in ended. On Easter Sunday 16 April 2006 friends pulled me out of the house and into town to party it up. My best friend Symone and her boyfriend Adam were part of the group, and so was Adam's good friend Sam.

Standing in the queue to get into the hotel, I was nervous and uncomfortable. Sam exuded confidence. Waltzing straight up to me, he had a game plan, and I could see it. The instant attraction was still there, although I wasn't interested. Sam had a reputation as being a ladies' man, and I wasn't about to play that game! But as he had recently returned from a year abroad we had plenty to talk about—if I could get a word in! The night ended much later after plenty of drinks, fun and laughter. It wouldn't be long until I saw Sam again.

I next encountered Sam at Adam's house. We were getting ready to go to the annual Wine and Seafood Festival, and Sam was part of the group. Again, the attraction was there, but still I maintained I wasn't interested (at least, that was my game plan and I was sticking to it). We caught a lift with a friend, and sat in the back seat together, Sam nudging in closely. I knew he was keen on me but thought it was just a bit of fun for him so I didn't play into his charm. Instead I challenged him. Our personalities were strikingly similar and talking to him was like being hit with a bigger version of myself. We glanced into each other's eyes, and I still remember thinking, 'Uh, oh. This is trouble. You're the male version of me!' We took a photo. I still have it to this very day, the first photo of us together.

It started to bucket down with rain as we hopped out of the car, and Sam pulled me under the verandah of a house to keep me dry. Deciding to challenge him, I grabbed his hand and pulled him out into the rain and we both ran the few streets to the festival in the downpour. He was very surprised that I was happy to get completely drenched, even though I'd done the typical girly thing and had spent ages doing my hair and make-up. Although I hadn't spent much time with Sam, we had lots to talk about, and I felt very safe and comfortable with him.

We drank and ate our way merrily through the night, meeting up with friends along the way. I ran into a guy I had briefly flirted with in the previous month. He was with another girl, so in mock revenge I grabbed Sam and kissed him! It was an odd first kiss but we were both nineteen years old—this is what you do when you're young. Sam kissed me back, and as short as it was we both knew there was something there.

Hours later, when we all returned to Adam's the beds and couches filled up quickly. Sam and I spent hours awake on a blanket in Adam's backyard chatting about life's little wonders under the stunning Queensland night sky. It was very cold, but that didn't matter. We happily laid there talking, when we saw a shooting star. 'This would be so romantic if it were with the right person', said Sam. I took this to be anyone but me, and unknowingly turned away as Sam tried to kiss me.

Nothing happened that night, but it didn't need to. It was old-school romance and the start of something bigger.

On 6 May we had our second and third and fourth kiss, and many more. Our romance blossomed, it was fast paced and full of life. There was no stopping us; we were two kids deeply in love and willing to do anything to be together.

On 9 May Sam took me to Mount Cootha to see the view over Brisbane. It was beautiful. As we stood on the viewing platform under the gazebo, Sam told me this is where he wanted to get married. From day one, we were a pair; life-long partners. Fifteen days after we started dating, we confessed our 'I love yous' to one another.

On 16 June 2006 Sam flew to New York to go back to summer camp for the second year in a row. After his first year, he loved it so much he had booked his second year immediately. Little did he know we would find each other in the meantime. Five weeks after we started dating, Sam began his three-month working US holiday. It was agony, and as in love as we were, we had our share of lovers' quarrels. Being half a world away wasn't easy, but we made it out the other side. We knew if we could make it through that, we could do anything.

Sam's first call to me after he arrived in New York was to say he was standing in front of a jewellery store. He had seen the perfect engagement ring, and thought of me. Five weeks in, we both knew we were meant to spend our lives together.

I inked my love for Sam on my hip. 'Love' it said in cursive writing, an ode to my favourite saying: 'The greatest gift in life is to love, and be loved in return.' When Sam came home in September, we returned to our fast-paced relationship.

Apart from his three months overseas, there was rarely a night Sam and I spent apart from the day that we started dating. We focused on finishing our university degrees and I worked full-time to save for a deposit on our first home.

On 8 May 2009, on our third anniversary, Sam took me out to dinner at the Point Restaurant in Sydney. We drank and ate as if we were millionaires, and then casually walked down to the harbour. It was the perfect end to a perfect day. Sam had shown me every possible sightseeing spot and we had lovingly enjoyed them all. But unbeknownst to me, the night wasn't over. Having blindfolded me and telling me we were late, Sam made me walk up a steep set of stairs, over a very long bridge, down another set of stairs and onto a boardwalk. I was giggling with excitement anticipating a boat trip on the harbour under the stars. As I felt the boardwalk under my new heels, Sam stopped, placed his hands on my hips, and knelt down. I knew as soon as his body shifted what was about to happen, and immediately burst into tears. I was so excited. I had waited and hoped this day would come, and here it was.

My tears flowed so heavily with happiness that I couldn't hear much of what Sam said. Then he asked me to take the blindfold off. As black mascara-stained tears fell down my face I heard 'Will you marry me?' I cried even harder, unable to see the beautiful man in front of me, or the ring!

'Sal . . . are you going to say yes?' Of course, of course! The stars were shining and we looked back on Sydney, embracing. It was the most beautiful and happiest moment of my life. The world was our oyster, and we were going to live it.

Our life accelerated, and at full pace. I finished my university degree and was working as a successful wedding coordinator. Sam was finishing university and was looking at full-time work. We had an engagement party three weeks after Sam asked me to marry him amid rumours I was pregnant (why else would we be rushing?) and we went into full force wedding planning. Sam got a job a few months later and we bought our first home, a brand new townhouse in a leafy inner Brisbane suburb. Life was busy, but wonderful. We had everything we had dreamed of. We felt like the luckiest young couple in the world.

Valentine's Day

♥

Sunday 14 February 2010. Valentine's Day. Our romance had been filled with beautiful gestures. During our courtship, Sam often left love notes or roses under the windscreen wipers of my parked car at the train station. These gestures eventually blossomed into poems and even songs. Sam had a way with words that was so touchingly beautiful, you got lost when he spoke.

It was unusual that this Valentine's Day Sam didn't have anything planned. I was working until 5 pm, and Sam was playing in a work-organised soccer game, raising funds and awareness for SIDS. I arranged with my boss to finish at 3 pm so I could spend some time with Sam, and texted him to see if he wanted to take the dogs to the beach for the afternoon. Sam was playing soccer so I didn't expect a quick reply. But I got one, within five minutes, at about 1 pm. And then another. I asked if he was OK, and got a text saying 'Can't drive and can't go to the beach, honey, I'm so sorry! Worst dehydration in a long time, two hours of soccer . . . have been with first aid people!'.

It was an unusually hot day and it was rare, but not uncommon, that Sam suffered from dehydration. Sam has the Delta F508 strain of cystic fibrosis, a lung condition which is quite serious but had never really affected him badly. He didn't allow it to affect him, and he was in perfect shape, as fit as an athlete. Dehydration is a common side effect of cystic fibrosis as the body's salt levels become low.

A few more texts were exchanged and I rang Sam to see if he wanted me to pick him up. He broke down on the phone, crying, saying he was in so much pain from leg cramps that he wanted to go to the hospital and get a drip (IV fluid). Sam has always been very aware of his body and knew something was wrong, and so did I. Still suspecting it was dehydration, I finished up at work and called Sam again. This time he said he might need an ambulance. I offered to call one, but he refused it so I jumped in the car and drove the twenty minutes to Newmarket Soccer Fields to pick him up.

By the time I arrived Sam seemed much better; although excessively sweaty, the cramping had been resolved. He had drunk about 6–7 bottles of fluid and eaten a piece of a sausage roll. We discussed taking him to the hospital as a precaution, even though he no longer wanted to go. He wanted to sit still for a while, and then go later. As he seemed quite clear and orientated, I wasn't too concerned.

Within twenty minutes, Sam suddenly began vomiting profusely, and complained of a terrible headache. It hit him hard, and fast. He quickly became disorientated, unable to follow commands, rocking back and forth grasping his head, and saying it was going to explode. We immediately called an ambulance.

The ambulance arrived and I relayed Sam's symptoms and his medical history to the ambulance officers, who seemed in no hurry and were blasting their rock music. They took their time organising Sam before I requested we go to the hospital, and they loaded him into the ambulance and off we went. In the ambulance, Sam became even more disorientated, not knowing the day or date, although remembering his name. I was calm and even called his parents to let them know we were going to hospital for rehydration.

The ambulance officer asked me if Sam's pupils were usually different sizes, and I said no. He explained that this could indicate bleeding on the brain, and rang ahead to let them know we were coming. He did not seem fazed, and made me feel at ease, even talking about his children along the way.

Sam was swearing and irritated, moving his arms and legs about. At this stage, he was not showing any obvious signs of stroke that I was aware of.

We arrived at the hospital emergency department and Sam was becoming increasingly out of it. I remember jumping out of the ambulance thinking they would rush him inside but they casually took their time, music still blaring, in no apparent hurry.

Once on the other side of the emergency doors, I looked at Sam. He appeared completely out of it. The ambulance officer pointed to a desk no more than one metre from us and told me I could check Sam in there. In the time I glanced at the desk and then back at Sam, he had passed out. Within an instant Sam was gone, so fast, I couldn't even see him in the long white corridor in the split second I turned around. Little did I know, he hadn't passed out, but had gone into complete respiratory failure.

The lovely triage nurse behind the desk asked me Sam's date of birth. The first sign I was in shock was being unable to tell her if Sam's birthday was on 20 or the 22 September; I just couldn't remember, or focus to tell her. She assured me I could see Sam in fifteen minutes and to sit in the waiting room. They would call me when they were ready.

I stood waiting, annoyed at Sam for not taking better care of himself on such a hot day, when they called me. I was greeted by a beautiful but 'sorry' looking social worker who didn't know what to say to me, but reassured me all the same. She took me down the long corridor to the family waiting room with lead-lined walls. I couldn't call anyone on my mobile because of the lead, and the social worker stayed with me for what seemed like hours, without being able to tell me anything. I knew then we were in trouble.

Although it felt like hours, Sam's parents and his oldest brother joined me in this little prison-like room shortly afterwards. I was shaking, feeling bizarrely out of it, almost like I was watching myself from somewhere else. It wasn't too much longer until the head of the emergency department came to explain what was happening. His face said it all, so he didn't need to talk. It didn't matter what he was saying, I knew this was as bad as it could get. He had the same look on his face that I would encounter nearly every single day for the next few years or so. A look of 'I am so sorry, you are too young for this'.

The doctor sat bravely, while Sam's parents and brother cried as he spoke. I sat quietly, shaking, listening, in a state of shock. He explained that they didn't know what was happening to Sam but that his pupils were indicating a significant bleed on the brain. They had been stabilising him to take him for an MRI scan, to see what damage there was, and to try to find a source for the bleed. The words didn't matter to me, I knew what was happening. We were then told that we could go and see him shortly, before he was transferred to the Intensive Care Unit (ICU). I understood at that moment, that when I had turned and believed Sam had passed out, he was in fact dying. They had rushed him into the resuscitation section of the emergency department, to bring him back to me.

As we left the private room, I followed closely behind the doctor and social worker. We rounded a corner and there he was, in a coma, criss-crossed by tubes. It was a scary sight, but seeing Sam with all of those tubes and machines didn't bother me, it was the expressions on the medical staff's faces. That told me he didn't have long to live. It was a look of 'sorry' and sorrow.

We only had a brief minute to kiss and cuddle Sam before he was transferred upstairs to ICU. His family gave me time to be with him; they knew how serious it was. I told him I'd see him soon, still not shedding a tear, and turned and walked away.

We were led down the corridor, and out of the emergency department. The social worker told us Sam could take a few hours to be transferred, as he was so unstable. She politely gave us directions, and off we wandered. Josh, Sam's brother, and I went outside; his parents, upstairs. Strangely, my thoughts were on practical matters such as our cars and our dogs. Our cars were in different locations and our dogs needed to be fed. The sun was starting to set, and so I made a phone call. I had previously called my mum from the ambulance to say we were heading in for suspected dehydration. My dad answered the phone, and there it was: that flood of tears that would fall from my eyes at the drop of the hat for a year or so after. I broke down, uncontrollably. All I could say was 'It's bad, Dad, it's so very bad.' Even then, I don't think he could understand me. He knew, from my tears, that it was serious. They arrived at the hospital shortly after, and organised all the practical matters. Dad went off to get our things together, and Mum stayed with me. My younger brother and his partner emptied their closets into suitcases that night and went to our house to look after the dogs. And there they stayed for the next month or more, devoted to us.

A few hours later we were allowed to see Sam, only two relatives at a time. There he was, hooked up to a dozen machines—his life hanging by a thread. All I could do was sit next to him, hold his hand, and cry. I couldn't stop; I cried for so many hours, just wishing he would get better. I couldn't fathom losing him, and so many questions came and went in my mind. I didn't leave the hospital for another six days. There I stayed, hoping, wishing, waiting.

Chapter 1

Sammy . . . a tale of a survivor

♥

At least I am only a few metres away from you. Day 5, and today I saw sunlight for the first time. Everyone has been encouraging me to have some 'me' time, assuring me if I go home, you will be OK. Truth be told, no-one understands. You are my life. You always have been. How could I leave you even for a minute?

The guilt I feel when I leave to even shower (in the hospital shower) is unbearable. I crave you. I crave your smell. Your laugh. Your touch. Every moment I get with you is heaven. Awake or not, I need to be there with you. I have always told you that; love is powerful.

The greatest gift in life is to be loved, and to love in return. And wow—are you loved!

Right now I am leaning on your upper leg. You look handsome. I'm pretty sure you're 'passing' something, as you just dropped a massive stinky. My head was in the direct firing line!

Your physiotherapist has just come to work on you. He is focusing on cleaning out your chest so when you choose to wake up, you won't cough too much. Too much coughing will increase your blood pressure, and in turn your ICP (Intercranial Pressure), which is the amount of pressure in your brain. Your vitals right now are:

♥ *Friday 19 February 2010, 3:40 pm*

BP:	129/84 (96) MAP
Pulse:	75
ICP:	11
CPP:	86
Temp:	38.2

You are coping amazingly!

For the last twelve or so hours, although still listed as 'critical', you are quite stable. They tell us, five days in, they just don't know what's wrong. You may have had a level 5 subarachnoid haemorrhage. However, there is something else which caused it. It is not the primary reason for your condition. The very rare genetic condition they think it is hasn't been seen at this hospital in two years.

The physio is done now, and he got lots of gunk off your lungs, which is great. You just vomited. Poor baby. They tell me an ENT doctor (Ears, Nose and Throat) is coming to see you today, to try and clear all the gunk up for you. The great ICU nurses have been working around the clock (24/7) to support you. They have been feeding you a nutritional supplement through a nose tube which goes into your belly. For the last two days you have vomited up everything fed to you. It looks identical to your beloved iced coffees, but I'm sure it doesn't taste as good! You look so beautiful. You have every tube imaginable in you, but you are still my Sammy G. Right now, you have the following things hooked up:

- *Ventilator (mouth)*
- *Feeding tube (nose)*
- *Brain tap (forehead and arm)*
- *BP reader (wrist)*
- *Pulse reader (finger)*
- *ECG monitor (chest × 5)*
- *Pressure socks (legs and feet)*
- *Leg pressurisers (legs)*
- *Ski boots (legs and feet)*
- *Catheter (willy)*
- *Drip (arm)*
- *Blood stealer (arm)*

I've just been asked to 'step-out' for 5–10 minutes, as they are 'padding up blueys' and giving you a laxative. I feel terrible for you because your tummy is so swollen and tight from not doing a poo. It's really quite painful, I'm told.

You're in bed 16, and as I've seen many patients come and go from ICU, mostly elderly, I've just looked over to bed 14, which has a young South Pacific-looking guy in it. He doesn't have anything attached to his head that I can see, but all his other apparatus looks similar to yours.

Our social worker just stopped in to see how I am coping. She is off for the weekend so we are assigned to a very butch-looking woman with grey, short hair.

I've just come back in to see you now; you're all 'blueyed' up and I told you about the Facebook page Toby set up for you. It's a page for everyone to leave messages of love so I can read them to you daily. He set it up at 9.52 this morning and already you have over 60 messages! (12 pm) In the last five days we have had an amazing amount of messages of love. I am not surprised by any means, as you are amazingly popular, incredibly loved and everyone's friend! You are a phenomenal person. A one-in-a-million fiancé, and I am so proud to say I am yours. I have so much faith in you, and so does everyone. There is a list of people who have been here *every single day* since Sunday (the day).

Bedside Vigil Crew
- ♥ *Me*
- ♥ *Joshie*
- ♥ *Your mum and dad*
- ♥ *My mum and dad*
- ♥ *Amanda and Jono*
- ♥ *Jake and Alyce*
- ♥ *Ritchie and Kate*
- ♥ *Matty*

Every day from around 6 am to 6 pm (except me, I've slept here every single night):
- ♥ *Viv and Leila (since Tues)*
- ♥ *Luke (Since Wed)*
- ♥ *Aunty Kardy (since Tues)*
- ♥ *Cate and Mike (since Tues)*
- ♥ *Symone and Adam (every day except Thursday)*

Other visitors who have been very, very consistent and come every day or 'just a bit' are:
- ♥ *John and Sandra*
- ♥ *Sharpie*
- ♥ *Louisa*
- ♥ *Michelle*
- ♥ *Steve*
- ♥ *Gerard*
- ♥ *Phil*
- ♥ *Kirsten (Josh's friend)*

- ♥ *Jono*
- ♥ *James and Lisa*

There are many, many more! I just can't think of them all.

Vitals ♥	*Friday 19 February 2010, 9.30 pm*
BP:	—
Pulse:	78
ICP:	—
CPP:	119
Temp:	38.6
BPM:	26 (set at 12)—Yellow—2nd

They are just putting in another heart line to measure your BP . . .

Darling. Another day is over. It's 12.20 am on Saturday 20 February, and Joshie and I are retiring to bed. We have spent each night here, sleeping in different locations, so the hospital staff don't find out and kick us out, like homeless people. Each night is as follows:

Sun 14th:	No sleep (1 hour in your room)
Mon 15th:	ICU small waiting room
Tue 16th:	Level 4 elevator bench
Wed 17th:	ICU meeting room
Thurs 18th:	ICU meeting room
Fri 19th:	ICU waiting room (at end)

I wish they would let me lie on your bed and snuggle up to you, but you're not well enough and I'm not allowed. Tonight you have a lovely ICU nurse, he is from Santa Fe, New Mexico, United States! He has been in Australia for four and a half years, and has three kids, aged eight, twelve and twenty-one years! I just found out the young bloke in bed 14 had an asthma attack. He is 19 years old. A woman from Perth and her sister from Bundaberg might stay overnight with us tonight; their mum is in bed 13 and has lung cancer.

I doubt Joshie and I will be allowed to sleep here any longer. Tonight might be our last night. I'm almost certain tomorrow night they will call security on us.

So far you have had four bunches of flowers delivered, so I have decorated the ICU waiting room with them. You aren't allowed anything in ICU as it can bring in infection. Anyway, I have to sleep to ensure I'm 100 per cent for you!

I LOVE YOU.

Sal xxx

DAY 6: SATURDAY 20 FEBRUARY 2010

Sammy is a warrior

Hi honey!

Today lots of people have visited already and it's only just gone midday!

- ♥ *Me*
- ♥ *Joshie*
- ♥ *Alyce*
- ♥ *Mum and Dad (mine)*
- ♥ *Amanda*
- ♥ *Lukie*
- ♥ *Liam*
- ♥ *Goldie*
- ♥ *Symone*
- ♥ *Leonie*
- ♥ *Jemma*
- ♥ *Alan*
- ♥ *Ian*
- ♥ *Aunty Melody*
- ♥ *Cate*
- ♥ *Mike*
- ♥ *Antonio*
- ♥ *Anthony M*

Today you are on the CPAP. *You are breathing on your own!* You still have the ventilator in your throat but it isn't switched on. We are thrilled. Oh! I just remembered—on Wednesday in our 'family meeting' with the doctor, we were looking at your MRI scans, and you really do have a big head! Ha ha! And a big—

LUMP!

Wow! It's now 9 pm and your Aunt Melody was just here. She drove five hours from Coffs Harbour to see you for half an hour before she had to catch her flight back to Sydney!

I'm currently trying to buck up the courage to go home and get some sleep tonight. It's going to be very hard leaving you and going home . . . without you. I'm just sitting by your bed and your ICU nurse is giving you some drugs to settle your tummy. It's almost three days since you have had a feed because your tummy and bowels had a 'blockage' and you kept vomiting. If you don't stop vomiting by Monday they will start feeding vitamins right into your bloodstream. Right now everything is a matter of balancing your medications to keep you settled enough for your brain to heal. It could take weeks, months or years. They just don't know.

DAY 7: SUNDAY 21 FEBRUARY 2010

Sammy is my soulmate

Morning, babe. It's 12.40 am and I can't sleep . . .

It's my first night at home without you and I *hate* it. I did a big clean-up of our bedroom to keep me occupied, but I'm sitting in bed and you're not next to me. I'm shattered and lost. I have been the rock through this. When everyone else has fallen apart around us, I have kept upbeat, positive and strong. I know it's the only way you would want me to be. But, at night, it is awful. Especially now, when I cannot lie next to you. I tried to stay as long as possible at the hospital, and got home at 10.10 pm. I had called the ICU by 11 pm to check on you. Still, nothing beats being with you. I feel safe when I am with you.

Jake and Alyce have moved in to help me. Work has been great, I'm taking *all* of my annual leave, sick leave and carer's leave (about three paid weeks) and then I will be on unpaid leave indefinitely. I am not returning to work until you also are ready to go back to work. I want to be there every single step of the way, and I can't imagine not being with you each day. I have just called the ICU *again*, to check on you. It's now 12.15 am and I feel sorry for the nurse as I have now called twice to check on you.

I am so positive and strong during the day but I am not coping at all being at home without you. I can't help but break down into tears every time I think about the amazing times we have had in our home, and that I can't feel you in bed with me. Ralph and George are sleeping in your spot. All I want is for you to open your eyes and recognise me.

Just recognise me.

AM.

Fuck. You had a bad turn last night. They tried to take you off the Propofol and put you on Fentanyl. Your body didn't like this. All of your pressures increased significantly and we came rushing into the hospital. They wouldn't let us see you until you were stable. I cried on your arm for half an hour. It's just not fair. Tragedy has struck all around us. It always does in ICU. I am not going to let this happen to us. Every time I struggle, you give me a little sign. A tiny little yellow curved line on your ventilator to show me that you're here, breathing and fighting. You are much more stable now, and are absorbing feeds. This is a good sign. You look so peaceful and beautiful. There is an elderly man named Douglas in bed 15 next to you, he is unsettled and trying to get the ventilator out. He is awake. When you wake up, I can't wait to see the life in your eyes.

Vitals ♥ *9.55 pm*

BP:	170/70
Pulse:	54
ICP:	22
CPP:	74
Temp:	36.8
BPM:	19–CPAP

Drugs

Mild Sedation
Fentanyl (120 ml)
Propofol (100 ml)

A massive accident occurred last night.

A guy fell off a cliff at Point Cartwright up the coast and his two mates fell off trying to save him. Two guys died and the other got evacuated to your ICU pod (2 of 4). I've seen his family all day and they have switched off his life support and are sitting with him until he passes. It's the third person to move to 'the other side' while you have been in here. Very sad.

Tonight is a small milestone for you. Seven days in, and not only are you breathing on your own, your vitals look amazing after the *third attempt* at switching you from Midazalom to Fentanyl. The last two times your body rejected it. *Wow.* I just felt a tap on my arm and *no-one* is close. The nurse is about three metres away. I have been feeling such positive spirits all around us in the hospital, and I truly believe *all* of our 'passed' grandparents and family are here watching over you. I asked Aunty Jane to tell all of our 'passed' relatives that if they see you coming, to stop you and tell you to go back. *I know it's not your turn yet.* Tonight Kim and Joshie (Jake's friends) gave us some wonderful things:

- ♥ *Quartz necklace (love and strength)*
- ♥ *Raffaello coin (courage, love and hope)*
- ♥ *Angel stone (hope)*

I ♥ you Sammy G

DAY 8: MONDAY 22 FEBRUARY

Sammy is strong

Well, I got home at 11.20 pm and it's now 12.24 am. So far I have cleaned the house, put on a load of washing and unpacked and packed the dishwasher. I am not settled. Luke offered to stay with you so I could sleep. I will be back at the hospital at 6 am, but how can I sleep without you? I called ICU to check on you, and once again your pressures have gone up so they have had to sedate you again. You are so heavily sedated you do not have the strength to breathe on your own. All I want to do is rush to ICU to be close to you. I am thinking about going to pick up your wedding ring tomorrow. I want to wear it on a chain, around my neck, but I don't want to have to leave the hospital to do this. I know your body, mind and spirit need time to recover but I am so anxious to have you moved to another ward. To do this, you will need to wake up, respond to commands, be alert, breathe on your own, and talk. You will then be listed as stable and be moved to a neurological ward. But after seven days you are still listed as 'critical'. We have not had enough time together in life, and I am praying with *all* my heart and soul that we are granted and blessed with more.

I love you, xxx

Vitals ❤ *9.30 am*

BP:	159/65
Pulse:	61
ICP:	19
CPP:	68
Temp:	37.2
BPM:	20 (set) all red

Drugs

Midazalom
Propofol
Fentanyl (heavily sedated)

DAY 9: TUESDAY 23 FEBRUARY

Sammy is my all . . .

Today has been a frustrating day. My body took over and physically crashed. I slept in til 7 am, which meant I wasn't at ICU until 8 am . . . !

I have only been having 3–5 hours' sleep, which is mostly interrupted. I just want to be by your side all day and night. It's now 7 pm and I have only seen you for a few hours today. We had a 'family meeting' with our social worker and the lovely doctor which took up most of the day.

They have now admitted you didn't have a bleed at all (or a subarachnoid haemorrhage) as they call it. You did have a grade 5 stroke, which is the worst, but they think you have an enzyme (metabolic) disorder, called mitochondrial disease.

This is a form of Melas which is a degenerative neurological disease. They will explain all of this to you when you wake up.

You look stunning tonight.

Anything could happen to you and I would still think you were the most amazing, handsome man in the world. So today has been very busy with meetings for you, and you've also had a chest x-ray, physio, and a bronchoscopy (where they go in and clear out your chest). You are showing signs of a slight chest infection in your lower left lung. They have put you on antibiotics.

Hopefully tomorrow they will perform a tracheotomy and put a tube in your throat for breathing.

Vitals	♥ 8.05 pm	
	BP:	162/70
	Pulse:	75
	ICP:	13
	CPP:	82
	Temp:	38.0
	BPM:	24 (set) all red
Drugs	Midazalom	
	Propofol	
	Fentanyl (heavily sedated)	

This will allow you to breathe without having the ventilator in your throat. It is obvious you hate the ventilator, and when they lower your sedation, the ventilator stresses you out. The stress then increases your pressures and they have to sedate you.

It's a vicious cycle.

So, you can see, although I'm here all day, I can't see you all day, due to all the tests. Today they also made some wrist splints for you so your wrists and hands don't curl up! Oh, and you're on 'infections alert' because the guy next to you, has VRE. That's one of those nasty superbugs that you hear of. Don't worry, you can only catch this by touching his faecal matter! Ha ha!

They are moving him into isolation but until they free up the isolation room and move him, we all must wear aprons around you. It's 8.45 pm and your brothers just left to get some sleep. Jake and Alyce just arrived . . . I have to leave at around 10.30 pm tonight, because Maartje arrives from Holland at 6.50 am tomorrow, and she is coming straight from the airport to ICU to see you. We will have a lot to catch up on, so I need the rest!

It's very, very hard for me when people see you for the first time. They are on emotional day one, and I am on day 9. I am so much stronger now, and watching them get so upset seeing you brings me down quite a bit. I try not to be around them then. I just can't take the chance of going back even a day with my emotions, I need to be strong for you.

♥

'Ever thine,
Ever mine.'

DAY 10: WEDNESDAY 24 FEBRUARY

Sammy is unique

'Morning, Sammy. You look beautiful today!'

That's what I say every single morning to you. This morning, it's a hive of activity at your bedside. You are having physio, suctioning and the trainee nurses are here also! You have your legs out, and all of your pressure socks and splints are off because they need to put a line in your foot. Your nurse today is a cool guy around our age who enjoys looking after you. He got married last year. You are scheduled in for a 10 am muscle biopsy (to test for Melas) and a tracheotomy. They also have some other tests to run so we won't be able to see you much today. Maartje arrives from Holland today, and is coming straight from the airport to ICU. She loves you very much. Luke (bro) goes to Adelaide this afternoon to see the kids, but will be coming back. Kardy leaves tomorrow! Wow, just found out you used to look after the nurse's wife's cousin! He can't remember his name but will find out for you!

Your new food is ready for you today, it's specifically formulated for cystic fibrosis patients. Due to your malabsorption you vomited up for days. Just found out your trachea might not be until Friday. Urgh. I really want this done ASAP. The earlier the better.

Your new food has Arginine in it, which is a vitamin they use to treat Melas. There isn't a real treatment for Melas, as it is so rare.

I just left your bedside and went home. Our dogs were thrilled to see me. I took a photo of them because Ralph is sleeping on your pillow. They really miss you. When I left you they were putting you back on Propofol due to your cough. You had been great this arvo, only having a small amount of Midazalom and Fentanyl. You were only moderately sedated and for the first time in a few days you moved!!!

I read out all of the Facebook messages, and you moved your arms, head and squeezed my hand! All of the nurses comment on how your vitals change when I'm around, and today you moved your legs quite a bit when you heard my voice. Our connection is so strong!

I am wearing your wedding ring on a chain around my neck. It gives me solace, and a goal to work towards.

I had to postpone the wedding today. It was a hard decision, but I know you wouldn't want to be in a wheelchair, or not 100 per cent at the wedding. The word is so strong now, even the wedding venue knew what had happened before my parents went in to meet them for me! Everyone is praying for you. I don't care when we get married, any moment I get to spend with you is bliss. Even if you're in ICU, coma and all, I don't care.

SAMMY, I LOVE YOU

I love you
No matter how you come.

I want to get your wedding band engraved with . . .

'Ever thine, ever mine, ever ours'

It is now 74 days before our original wedding date of 8 May 2010. That will be a hard day, but as long as we are together, I am happy. You're my everything . . .

xx

Vitals	*9 am*	
BP:	120/50	
Pulse:	76	
ICP:	11	
CPP:	57	
Temp:	37.6	
BPM:	25 (set) all red	
Drugs:	Midazalom	
	Propofol	
	Fentanyl	

DAY 11: THURSDAY 25 FEBRUARY

Sammy is a fighter

Hello, honey! You look as handsome as ever today. It's another busy day . . . you had a CT scan this morning. Charan and Rea are on level 5 today (we are on level 4) because Rea is in labour! So exciting! It's a little boy and they are naming him Adrian! Well, again I didn't get to see you much . . . they did a lung x-ray this morning and a CT scan. *Amazing news*! Your CT scan showed improvement! Honestly, that is the first big decent news we have heard in the last eleven days. I am overwhelmed. Tomorrow is your tracheotomy and they might also be taking out your EVD (brain tap). The cranial pressures that we have all been terrified would cause you further brain damage every time they increased do not need to be increased after all! I highly suspect they would have tried to wake you up days ago if they had not been measuring the intercranial pressure. The word 'NOB' comes to mind now. Oh well . . . you are in the best possible hospital for neuro. It's now bedtime, and our puppies are all snuggled up on your side of the bed asleep. George has been sick today, vomiting and not eating. Poor fellow, eating too many rocks from the garden again! Well, you will be really annoyed because I had the dryer running a *lot*!

I haven't been home or had time to hang the clothes out, so I have been using the tumble dryer. I'm sorry if the energy bill is a bit higher than usual. Oh! I rang the bank today, and they have a 'hardship' department, should we get into any financial difficulty. We should be OK for a while.

I don't plan on going back to work for a few months, until you are awake, stable and happy for me to do so. I plan on being your full-time carer. Lucky I used to work as a carer for kids with disabilities!

Tonight you had some Coca-Cola . . . they put some down your feeding tube to erode any blockages. Goes to show how bad it is for you!

I can't wait to see you tomorrow; my entire life is lying in that hospital bed, I just want to be near you . . .

I love you.

xx

DAY 12: FRIDAY 26 FEBRUARY

Sammy is a trouper

Ugh. Bad day. You have pneumonia. This is not good. It is so bad that they are no longer focused on the Melas. Right now, all they are focused on is treating your condition clinically (as it presents). Pretty much the pneumonia could be the end. You will be lucky to survive. Your body isn't responding very well to the antibiotics. Like everything else that has happened, I know you will beat it. After all, you are a trouper. They took your EVD (brain tap) out today.

You are not having a tracheotomy today now. They are too 'scared' to do this until your pneumonia is gone. The head-honcho is having a 'family meeting' with us today. So far we have spoken with all of the other doctors, but not the head guy. I'm not sure if this is a good thing.

Today I am angry . . . At the world . . .

So the family meeting was OK. Everything we must take with a grain of salt, as anything can change at any time, and it is still very much touch-and-go.

For the first time we have had a glimmer of hope!

All of the information on the internet states that Melas is a degenerative neurological disease, which it is. It also says it is fatal. The doctor, however, said, and I quote: 'We would not be treating him if we did not think he would recover.'

I almost *fell* off my chair. I mentioned a few days ago they are treating you with Arginine . . . (I'll explain Melas) . . . Melas covers five types of Melas, the first being mitochondrial. Mitochondria are the 'batteries' to your enzymes, which make the body function. Melas is a metabolic syndrome. So by treating the metabolism enzymes with arginine, it flows through the body and 'recharges' the enzymes!

The reality check that the professor gave us, though, is that if it is *not* Melas, they are in 'unchartered territory'.

He did also say that the paediatric neurologist advised not to wake you up until at least three weeks after your admission . . . so we have another ten days until that.

Vitals	♥	9.40 pm	
		BP:	123/46
		Pulse:	72
		CVP:	12
		Temp:	38.0
		BPM:	23 Yellow (pressure not forced)
Drugs		Midazalom	
		Propofol	
		Fentanyl	

DAY 13: SATURDAY 27 FEBRUARY

Sammy is a golfer

Well Sammy, I've been reading lots to you! *Zen Golf*; *Golf Digest* and a new book of Ritchie's called *My Little Red Book*—also a golf number. I've also been reading the sports section of the paper, just something I knew you would like! As usual, I'm totally in love with you. I swear you're even more handsome each time I look at you . . .

I love you.

I've been massaging you with body moisturiser twice a day to ensure you don't dry out, and to try and keep the fluid moving. Today I noticed you've lost quite a bit of muscle mass in your arms and legs, which happens. Your temperature is high, but that's all part of the fever from pneumonia.

I can't wait til you wake up.

Sal xxx

DAY 14: SUNDAY 28 FEBRUARY

Sammy the man

Hello, darling! Well this morning you had a *very* high temperature of 39.9! That is huge. You also weren't producing enough CO_2, so they spent one and a half hours changing your ventilator mode over to fix this. Not producing enough CO_2 on your exhale can be 'toxic,' or 'fatal' (a word I have heard enough of in this lifetime). Symone and Adam just came to visit. They, as everyone does, love you a lot. I'm writing this on your bed, watching you. You look so peaceful. You're all swollen again, as the fluids pool in your body. You're nice and stable now, though, as they changed your antibiotics. I'm hoping the worst of the pneumonia is over. I can't wait until they do the tracheotomy and they attempt to wake you. It will be a terrifying, emotion-filled, yet beautiful day.

Vitals	♥	9.35 pm	
		BP:	97/65
		Pulse:	78
		CVP:	20
		Temp:	37.8
		BPM:	20 (APRV/B/Phasic) pressure mode
Drugs		Midazalom (D/S)	
		Fentanyl (D/S)	

You could wake up normal; mentally disabled (to what extent we don't know) or, not at all. I need more time with you. I just don't feel like this is the end. It can't be. We are too young and our lives together are only just beginning. I want the best for you, but I want and need you. All I can do is pray, hope and wish you wake up, as my Sammy. I take solace in the fact that no matter what, you will choose the right thing for us. Whether it be you passing or staying, I know you and only you will make that choice. And I have peace with that. I know that deep down, if you didn't want to live, no amount of 'life support' machinery could keep you here. The fact you are defying all the odds fourteen days on shows me you want to stay and fight. The next few days, months and years will be a hard and long fight. I am, and always will be, fighting with you, by your side. My entire life is lying here right in front of me, in critical condition. And I will do anything and everything to make it stable again.

You are my life source, my breath, my heartbeat, my soul.

I love you.

Sal xxx

Vitals   *Too scary to record.*

DAY 15: MONDAY 1 MARCH

Sammy is a legend

Legend you are and always will be. The number of people at your 'Drinks for Sammy/ICU fundraiser' at the pub tonight is amazing! A local legend, inspiration, and golf tragic you are known as! ♥ ♥ ♥

> *Where to start . . . as you all know, on Sunday 14 February, our life was shattered.*
>
> *Given minute chances of survival, Sammy has continually beaten the odds. From initially surviving, to surviving the first 24 hours, to defying the doctors, and surviving the first ten days.*
>
> *It is inevitable, and undoubtable, that these miracles could not have occurred without the love and support shown by each and every one of you here tonight, and countless others around the world. Sammy is one loved guy.*

Sammy and I cannot thank you enough for the wonderfully kind, loving support you have given. Each and every one of your hopes, wishes and prayers have come together to create one big, beautiful support network. We have been continually blown away by how touching your words, experiences and wishes have been.

It takes one beautiful soul like Sammy to connect with so many individual, generous and loving people as yourselves.

I sit here, at Sammy's bedside, looking at that beautiful soul, recounting all of those messages of support. Every now and then, when I least expect it, I get a little twitch, a hand squeeze, an eyelid flicker, to let me know he is listening.

The dire straits around us will not get us down, and true to Sammy's form, all challenges are possible.

All we can do is stay positive and strong, and live each day as if it were our last, much as Sammy always has. In his words: 'Back yourself, Tiger.'

We cannot predict the future, but I can tell you this . . . Sammy would want this to be a war story. A tale of survival, much as his other adventures have been. He is a true fighter.

Sally

Darling . . . today has been a particularly hard day. Your pneumonia is 'roaring'. It is very, very bad. You are not even 'stable' enough within your critical listing to have an MRI, as the sheer movement involved in taking you is too risky.

We have been told the next two to three days are as crucial as the first 24 hours were . . . in other words, your chance of survival is minimal.

The head doctor's protégé has told us he does not believe it is Melas, and believes it was a subarachnoid haemorrhage. So two different ideas, stories and conclusions to contend with now. I'm really starting to become emotionally fucked. I feel numb to all of the pain, and then immense guilt because of the numbness. Today they told us you have 'advanced cystic fibrosis' . . . something quite shocking considering how little it has affected your life. They say you are extremely lucky, and it's a 'miracle' that you have not been sicker, considering the state of your lungs. I'm angry.

I'm so fucking angry this has happened to us. It's not fair. You have been a tremendous person all your life, and now, in a shockingly cruel twist of fate, this. Everything is one big, nasty roller-coaster. Your lungs are so bad, they are struggling to ventilate you. It's now a matter of your brain and your lungs battling it out. They need to ventilate you more, so you can get enough CO_2, but this increases brain pressure, and then further brain injury.

The doctor said, 'It's a matter of either blowing a hole in his lung, or blowing his brains out.'

I officially hate life. What is life without you? Still, I cannot see the end, I cannot imagine this ending 'badly'. I want so bad to fix you, or take your place.

All I can do is take solace in the fact that you will make the right choice for us, to stay, or go.

DAY 16: TUESDAY 2 MARCH

Sammy, my fiancé

Another awful day. I have a dress fitting, and have no idea how I will try on the wedding dress I may never wear, let alone pick it up and take it home, to hang in our bedroom . . .

Well, I did well. I took Mum, Aunty Jane and Jake with me and my dress looks amazing. I cannot wait to wear it on our wedding date, whenever that shall be.

You had an awful night last night. Joshie and I stayed the night as they gave you a 50/50 chance of surviving it. It was so scary! I was talking to you and your heart rate jumped from 97 to 162 in a millisecond. Your normal resting heart rate is 52 . . . All the doctors and nurses came rushing over and I was ushered out. I thought it was the end. This happened again at about 4 am, but as before, your heart rate quickly dropped back to 97. It was *beyond* frightening.

Chapter 2

Sam is INVICTUS . . . unconquered

♥

Live as if tomorrow is your last day
Sing as if no one is listening
Love as if you have never been hurt
From your brother Joshie, to keep me smiling

DAY 19: FRIDAY 5 MARCH 2010

Sammy the show-off

Oh, Sammy . . .

Well, I haven't written the last two days. It wasn't worth it. We had a family meeting yesterday, and the doctor said: 'The pneumonia is out of control. He has a 10 per cent chance of surviving the pneumonia. I'm so sorry.'

These words will forever ring in my head. They didn't think you would live. It is not the worst odds we have been given. The lowest was 5 per cent, so you can bet we are hanging onto the 10 per cent like it were our own life. Everyone came in to see you, to tell you to fight on. You survived the night.

Joshie and I stayed the night. There was no way we could leave you. I cried for about two hours. Why is life so unfair? Why eight weeks before our wedding? Why us? Why you? All these questions ran through my mind again and again. The one thing I do know is we haven't had enough time together. Albeit the time we have had has been beautiful, just as you are. As amazing as you are, you beat the odds again last night. The doctor said they had done everything they could, and that it was up to you now. You are beyond sedated. So much so, you don't even have a chance to fight. You are unable to do anything for yourself. Not even cough. And just as your nurse told me this, then this very morning . . . *you coughed.*

You little bugger, you little show-off! Just another sign you are listening, and telling me you're still here, fighting on. You have had five bronchoscopies in the last 24 hours, and are having one now. They put an instrument into your chest, via your ventilator, and scrape the pus secretions off your lungs. It's nasty and risky, and they can only take you off the ventilator for two minutes without killing you (literally).

You are so strong. I love you.

Sal

DAY 19: FRIDAY 5 MARCH 2010 TO . . .

Vitals ❤	BP:	180/78
	Pulse:	111
	Temp:	37.7
	BPM:	24 (set) all red
Drugs	Midazalom	
	Fentanyl	

- ❤ *new breathing machine*
- ❤ *not breathing on own*

DAY 20: SATURDAY 6 MARCH 2010

Sammy is strong

Darling, another poo-tube! Lucky you. You have the runs, I feel for you. They are pumping laxatives into you so not your fault!

Well, last night the doctor told me you have a hole in your heart, nothing major. Most people have it from birth (one in four people) and it doesn't affect them. Now, with all of the drugs they have you on, it is causing you to have the odd irregular heartbeat. I'm just going to imagine it's your heart fluttering when you hear my voice.

Well . . . we are still getting the usual '10 per cent at best of surviving the pneumonia' talk. Fuckers. For those who know you, and know you well, we know that figure is only a challenge for you to beat. You have beat every figure so far, so we know you're a cheeky bugger whose competitiveness will show them all! The respiratory team seem to think you won't make it in the coming days, mainly due to your 'gas exchange'. This is when you breathe, the CO_2 levels are near-fatal, at 110 per cent. Today they are at 70 per cent. I asked you three hours ago to work on your CO_2 and now it's 65 per cent . . . I'm so proud. You just have to keep these little improvements up, and next week the neurology team will be waking you up, after your tracheotomy. They will be assessing your brain damage when you wake up. There is still no clear diagnosis, three weeks in. The doctors still believe it's Melas. The neurological radiologist won't change his initial diagnosis of subarachnoid haemorrhage. I, and the doctor, believe it is most likely an ischemic stroke (a stroke with no identifiable cause) most likely to be caused by a PDO (hole in heart). So many theories and no evidence.

Sal xxx

Vitals ♥ *7.50 pm*

BP:	152/84
Pulse:	121
CVP:	22
Temp:	37.5
O_2:	65%
Controlled breathing by ventilator.	

Drugs	Midazalom (D/S): 20 mg/hour
	Fentanyl (D/S): 14 mg/hour
	Vecuronium: 5.00 ml/hour
	Trobramison (antibiotic)

DAY 21: SUNDAY 7 MARCH 2010

Vitals ❤	*10.40*
	BP: 121/65
	Pulse: 114
	CVP: 11
	Temp: 38.0
	O_2: 55%
	Assisted breathing!!
Drugs	Midazalom (D/S): 20 mg/hour
	Fentanyl (D/S): 14 mg/hour
	* no muscle relaxant
	Trobramison (antibiotic)

DAY 22: MONDAY 8 MARCH 2010

Sammy the hunk

Well, darling, after peeing out eight litres of fluid overnight, you look back to your beautiful, handsome, hunky
self! Before you were so bloated even your eyelids looked
massively swollen.

Well, you are making improvements, albeit small ones. Your chest x-rays show your pneumonia is clearing, and your physio and bronchoscopies are being cut back because you don't require them as much. They aren't getting much pus and secretions up so that's a good sign. Your oxygen is down to 40 per cent, which is awesome (21 per cent = normal).

We had a gloomy bedside briefing with the doctor today . . .

Pretty much he told us they need to take your ventilator out and put in a trachea ASAP. The ventilator is only meant to be in for 7–10 days, and we are at day 22 . . . Not good. However, your lungs aren't strong enough for the tracheotomy. Great . . . he said, either you show significant improvement over the next two days, and you get a trachea, or, they take the ventilator out, leaving you with no way to breathe, which means goodbye, Sammy G. Not an option. We are all getting stuck into you to pull your socks up. I know you will. Why would you defy every single odd this far and then quit at the last minute? If they do the trachea, it will take 7–10 days for the sedation to wear off, and they'll assess your neurological abilities/damage. The worst part is, I know you're still in there, fighting for a way out, but if they turn your life support off, you have no way of fighting. I really feel like you need more time to prove yourself, so if you are given the trachea you can then show them you're still here in 7–10 days after the sedation wears off. How cruel to let you die without even assessing your neurological abilities. Doesn't seem right to me. I am in your corner, fighting hard. I am your voice right now, fighting for life.

I love you.

Sal xxx

DAY 23: TUESDAY 9 MARCH 2010

Sammy the surprise

Good morning, darling! Well, don't you look handsome today! You know you do. You're just having physio and I've just read you a beautiful email from Ant. Your boys really love you, Sammy. Steve is flying in from Perth to see you at Easter, Vic will be here in two weeks to see you from New York, and Dan, his missus Lucie and Rich will be here in May from the UK. Oh, and Steve just texted me saying he is flying in this weekend also to visit you! Well, it's been a busy day and as usual you have surprised us! All your vitals are looking good, your lungs have 'significantly improved'—the doctor's words—and you continue to improve every hour/day/ week. Today you were stable enough to move for an MRI, and the scans show that your 'brain damage' is the same as on the scans taken when you first came in, three weeks ago . . .

So they have reduced your sedations by around 15 per cent and will be closely monitoring your lungs' abilities tonight, in the hope they are strong enough for a tracheotomy tomorrow. We really hope we can get the trachea for you, because it buys more time to 'wake' you. They say it could take 7–10 days for all of the drugs to wear off and for them to be able to do a 'neurological' assessment of you.

I'm ready. Are you?

Well, surprise you do. I just leant down and whispered in your ear, and told you I love you, that I accept any choices you make for us. I told you I'd always fight, I'd never stop fighting for you. I asked you to show me a sign to let me know that you're still fighting for us, for our love, for life, and that you still love me. You made the most beautiful, clearest, purposeful eye and eyebrow squint I have seen to date. It feels so precious I can't share it. I feel immense love and peacefulness. That was your way of telling me everything will be OK, and I trust you.

I love you.

Sal xxx

Vitals ♥ *11 pm*

BP:	164/72
Pulse:	132
CVP:	11
Temp:	37.4
O_2:	35% (PEEP)

Drugs:

Midazalom (D/S):	18 mg/hour
Fentanyl (D/S):	10 mg/hour
Trobramison (antibiotic)	

DAY 24: WEDNESDAY 10 MARCH 2010

Sammy, unconquerable

Every time I look at you I open up my soul and fall so fast, your love, my love, our love . . . it will always survive. Nothing can tear us apart; our love will pull us through. When I sit with you, I forget all of the bad, I just feel unconditional love.

You're amazing, strong, unique. You fight to the brink of death and back. There is one word that truly defines you, and it was sent in a beautiful poem on Facebook by Toby . . .

INVICTUS

It means unconquerable in Latin. When this is all said and done, you deserve this word as a tattoo. Simple and proud, it is a true reflection of you.

Our love is unconquered.

Right now, you're having a skin check as part of the hospital's annual ulcer checks. The whole hospital gets done. You're also being turned over so your blood circulates properly, you don't get ulcers, and to enhance your breathing.

Oh, my, gosh. You have just had your tracheotomy, and it was a success! You look great, and I can kiss you on the lips now, at which I'm sure you're thinking, 'Get off me—Sal!'

I'm sitting by your bedside and you are phenomenal. Amazing. Truly inspiring. Again, unconquerable.

The doctor has just told us you're going as well as expected, however, your neurological responses to date are a 3 on the Glasgow Coma Scale (GCS). On the scale, a 3 is the worst and a 15 is the best. So . . . as you see, another down. Tomorrow will be a high, a low etc. Our love will survive.

* NOTE: A 20 per cent reduction in sedation will occur each day until you declare yourself.

I love you.

Sal xxx

Vitals ♥	9.45 am	6 pm
BP:	124/63	131/64
Pulse:	88	98
CVP:	3	—
Temp:	37.2	37.7
O_2:	30%	30%
PEEP:	8 cm H_2O	8 cm H_2O
Assisted breathing		—

Drugs:		
Midazalom (D/S):	18 mg/hour	14 mg/hour
Fentanyl (D/S):	10 mg/hour	8 mg/hour
Trobramison (antibiotic)		—

DAY 25: THURSDAY 11 MARCH 2010

Sammy the spunk

Guess who thinks you're a spunk? The nurses! Now that the ventilator is out and the tracheotomy is done, and they can see your face, the nurses all say how good looking you are! I knew this *all* along!

You're being a lazy little bugger for the doctor, not doing what he asks you. But when I say, 'Sam, squint your eyes/move your mouth/eyebrows,' you do it for me. You have reflexes in all of your limbs, so you're not 'paralysed', which is good. It's just up to you to start to move, open your eyes, poke your tongue out, squeeze my hand—this is what the doctors need to see. You're still quite heavily sedated, though, so we aren't expecting too much from you. My mum is all thrilled, well chuffed, because you squinted your eyes and moved your eyebrows for her this morning when she asked you!

I've just come back from dinner and I went to kiss you and you pulled your head away! Ha ha ha ha! Just like our first date, you cheeky bugger. Lying under the Queensland night sky after the Wine and Seafood Festival '06'!

Hmmm, how I miss those carefree uni days, and all the wonderful, naughty, spontaneous things we used to do! You, always looking so handsome, so full of confidence, a huge ego, lots of 'go'! Ha ha. I loved all of our dates, Mount Cootha, ice-skating, movies, rock climbing! You were always so thoughtful and considerate when choosing a date for us. And then there was the Marriott and Jade Buddha! What a night!

I love you.

Sal xxx

Vitals	❤ *1.20 pm*	
	BP:	126/66
	Pulse:	96
	CVP:	6
	Temp:	37.0
	O_2:	30%
	PEEP:	8 cm H_2O
	Assisted breathing, every fourth spontaneous	
	GCS:	3
Drugs	Midazalom (D/S): 10 mg/hour	
	Fentanyl (D/S): 5 mg/hour	

DAY 26: FRIDAY 12 MARCH 2010

Sammy the super

Super you are . . . the sedation, although only on a lower dose, is wearing off. You wiggled your toes, squeezed the doctor's hands, had facial expression, and your eyes are 'tracking'. The doctors are impressed. You are super Sammy!

It's been a huge day for you. I tired you out early on asking you to do things for me, so you slept for about 5–6 hours afterwards.

I've come home at 7.30 pm tonight to get some rest for a big weekend with you. You were so tired when Amanda and I left, and we didn't want to over-stimulate you. You are progressing so well, Sammy. So well. You're still sedated, although only about a quarter the amount. It's now 11.46 pm and I can't sleep, because at 4 am they will be switching off your sedation. It will run through your liver and kidneys until Tuesday, but we should see you 'wake up'. It's a very real concern that you may not, but I know you fight so hard. Tonight you responded to our questions by squinting your eyes. I asked you if you were comfortable, and to squint if you weren't. You did a huge squint. The nurse asked you if you wanted to lie on your back, sure enough, you squinted. We asked you if you were in pain, big squint. The nurse asked if you were born in 1986, you slightly shook your head no! I cannot wait to be by your side tomorrow as you become more conscious. I just hope you remember me. You did kiss me back today, five times! I thought I was imagining it! I love you.

Sal xxx

Vitals ❤	9.15 am		9 pm
BP:	126/64		126/64
Pulse:	102		84
CVP:	5		—

Temp:	37.3	36.7
O$_2$:	30%	30%
PEEP:	8 cm H$_2$O	6 cm H2O
Assisted breathing, every third spontaneous		1 hour breathing without machine!
CPAP (ventilator switched off) —breathing on own from 4 pm		
GCS:	8	12

Drugs	Midazalom (D/S): 5 mg/hour	NONE!
	Fentanyl (D/S): 5 mg/hour	

DAY 27: SATURDAY 13 MARCH 2010

Sammy . . . soulmate

Patience is not my virtue, Sammy. I've come to the hospital as early as possible, so I can see you. They turned off all of your sedation at 4 am this morning, and I'm so incredibly anxious to see your progress . . . I am imagining you'll only be slightly more responsive than last night, but that excited me. So many questions . . . Do you remember me? What happened? Are you OK mentally? I've been asked to wait ten minutes while the doctor finishes his assessment on you. I don't want to wait! I miss you so much, soulmate.

Today is going to be a big, momentous day. Please be OK.

* * *

Well, who is looking extra handsome this morning, slowly 'waking up'???? You're there, you just can't talk, open your eyes all the way, or have fluid movements. You're doing well, though! I asked you to raise your eyebrows if you love me—you did. On your own accord you then followed up by pursing your lips . . . ever so romantic! So I kissed you! I asked you if you would like me to read the *Australian Golf* mag to you—you squinted your eyes! It's been a very busy day for you . . . I've limited visitors to family and Ritch, Antonio, Goldie and Matty. Now that is still a lot of visitors. Because you're awake, it's much more exhausting for you to have people around. It's a lot of activity. We are seeing amazing signs from you. Even the doctors, who saw you on admission, told me to celebrate. 'It's amazing', they said! I asked one to get you to the wedding in eight weeks—and he said, 'Maybe—you never know.' Today you even sat up in a chair, with a lot of assistance. I imagine you won't remember this 'waking up' process. Still, you cannot move your eyes, but you are blinking to shadows, so I know you can see.

I love you.

Sal xxx

Vitals ❤	8.30 am		8.00 pm
BP:	145/72		173/69
Pulse:	87		73
CVP:	0		0

Temp:	38.4	37.4
O$_2$:	30%	—
PEEP:	5 cm H$_2$O	—
CPAP (breathing on own)		
GCS:	13	—

Drugs   NONE!

DAY 28: SUNDAY 14 MARCH 2010

Sammy, warrior! Hear me roar

Hello, handsome. You're asleep and you look every single inch my beautiful, intelligent, generous, loving husband-to-be. Boy, oh boy, won't our wedding be a true celebration of life !?!? You have so many supporters, so many loving friends, that over 300 people want to come to our wedding! We will have to have it in a church now, to thank God for this truly amazing miracle. Not only that, but the wedding venue isn't big enough for the ceremony now!

Well . . . you've got another chest infection! Bloody pseudomonas, they love you. Your cystic fibrosis makes it infinitely worse, although lying on your back for 24 hours a day doesn't help! They rotate you side to side, although nothing is quite like a big Sammy cough. OK, the nurse has just informed me your temperature climbed, you went hypertensive (blood pressure climbed) and you became unresponsive . . . another step back. This happens. Two steps forward, one step back. The doctors don't seem too concerned, you're exhausted so this is not uncommon. However, coupled with your previous pneumonia, I don't like the sound of it!

You really need to rest but all of the activity around you (doctors, nurses, patients, general noise) is keeping you awake. I know you need a big 12-hour sleep to prepare yourself for tomorrow. You also need to let your body rest and heal that nasty chest infection! You're adorable; you keep trying to talk to me, but the tracheotomy doesn't allow any sound to escape. Except when you're coughing! All the staff are super-impressed with your big cough. Tomorrow you really need to start showing the doctors what you're made of! It really all depends on you. Fight the infection, respond more, and they will start to think about moving you to a ward. Then we can all relax a little, and not live on edge. Every time the phone rings I jump out of my skin!

I love you.

Sal xxx

DAY 29: MONDAY 15 MARCH 2010

Sammy . . .

Darling, today's not a good day so I won't write much. You have deteriorated, a lot. From a 13 on the Glasgow Coma Scale, to a 7. The doctors are worried, so they have put another brain tap in to drain fluid off your brain. You also have pneumonia again, and a whole body infection. Again, 29 days in, there is no diagnosis, which is not good. I'm not coping today. I just want you back.

I love you.

Sal xxx

DAY 30: TUESDAY 16 MARCH 2010

Sammy the fighter

Surprise, surprise! You're showing everyone what a little character you are. Just like the Shambala warrior in *Zen Golf* (which I am reading to you), you possess all the right virtues. I am so proud of you. You were so stable today they were able to put you on a 'tilt-table', which moves you so you are simulating standing up. You're poking your tongue out again, and this morning you attempted to smile. Still, you need rest, and it's one baby step at a time. It's now 8.20 pm and I've just put on a little Jack Johnson. My theory is it slowly brings you out of your semi-conscious state into a wakeful state, nice and peacefully. Would be even better if it triggered a loving memory which then woke you. You're still not 'waking' like you should have by now, and all the nurses, doctors and professors are stumped, not to mention very worried. I'm trying to be as patient as possible, but as you can imagine, it's quite hard after 30 days, no diagnosis, no real treatment, and one million ups and downs. Also, I'm not a naturally patient person. I just love you so incredibly much, it's just so tremendously hard to see you like this, and to have to be 'real' and start to imagine that life may never be the same and that I may never have you back. As always, our love will prevail. I love you.

Sal xxx

Vitals	❤	*8.20 pm*	
		BP:	130/65
		Pulse:	85
		ICP:	8 (10–15 = normal)
		Temp:	37.0
		O_2:	30%
		PEEP:	5 cm H_2O
		CPAP (breathing on own)	
		GCS:	8
Drugs		Antibiotics × 4 types	
		Anticonvulsion meds	
		Midazalom × 5 ml boulis	

DAY 31: WEDNESDAY 17 MARCH 2010

Sammy the mighty

Last night I asked both of our guides (yes, spiritual guides), to show me a sign of what may lie ahead in our path together.

I also asked them to take you swiftly and quietly, if it is your time. Patience, guidance, protection, and strength—that's what I asked them to give us both.

You slept almost nine hours today, after only 'resting' from Saturday to Wednesday morning. When you woke tonight, at about 5.30 pm, you woke with might. You obeyed commands; poking out your tongue, squinting eyes, squeezing hands. It was phenomenal. Still, your GCS is only 8, but I can see the fight in you. It's almost like you needed a big sleep to regain your strength . . . the strength I asked our guides to give us. We are truly blessed, I can feel our guides all around us. I know last week you were floating above your body, deciding if it were your time. I could see and feel it. As Luke tells the kids, you were negotiating with God. I know our guides told you to go back, it wasn't your time, and I can feel them at your bedside, protecting you. It's all up to you. I'm playing Ben Harper as we have good memories together from that concert! You really do need to keep showing everyone how amazingly strong you are, your fight for life. I will not ever leave your side. Ever. I am here to battle life out with you, even if it means me being your full-time carer.

I am committed to you, in any capacity you come. Eternal life will always happen, as will eternal love. Even if we meet again on the other side, I will always feel you standing by my side. I am ready to embrace you again, feel your warmth, touch, strength, see your smile, your

effervescence for life. I am ready to spend the rest of our
lives together.

I love you.

Sal xxx

Vitals	♥	*8.05 pm*	
		BP:	137/61
		Pulse:	89
		ICP:	8
		Temp:	36.7
		O_2:	30%
		PEEP:	5 cm H_2O
		CPAP	
		GCS:	8
Drugs		Antibiotics × 4 types	
		Anticonvulsion meds	

DAY 32: THURSDAY 18 MARCH 2010

Samuel Lawrence

We just don't know what to do, neither do the doctors.
Today you're worse than yesterday. It seems as if every day
we go backwards. You should be ready and willing to start
showing signs of waking up. Apparently all the things you're
doing are things that people in a persistent vegetative state
do. And here we were getting so excited, thinking you were

going to be OK. I am starting to get worried, and I'm really, really frightened. I don't want you to be a 'vegetable'. I know you wouldn't want this. I'm scared if the MRI shows you're worse, and if you don't improve, they'll ask us to switch off your life support. How are we supposed to do that when you showed on Saturday you were in there? It's frightening.

I love you.

Sal xxx

DAY 33: FRIDAY 19 MARCH 2010

Sammy, fight!

Sammy, what a night last night! Your right lung collapsed! You had a pneumothorax (drain) put in, and it's doing well. The doctor says it's more of a nuisance than anything! You're still not really improving, which is not good. You had an MRI today which didn't show any changes in your brain . . . the damage is still high. After seeing them, the doctors have now said you have had EIGHT strokes—EIGHT. You don't do anything by halves do you, Sam? We have been told they want to put you on TP (no manual ventilation) and move you to the neuro/stroke ward. After one month there we will know if you will have a good quality of life or if we have to say goodbye . . . I love you.

Sal xxx

DAY 34: SATURDAY 20 MARCH 2010

I am Sam, hear me roar

Your lung has healed nicely and they took the lung drain out this morning. You look like your usual, gorgeous self lying there. They are trialling you on TP today: high-flow ventilator; it's more of an exercise to build up your muscles. It is imperative you do this 24/7 soon; it's your only way to the neuro/stroke ward. OK . . . so you didn't do well on the TP! Damn it. They were hoping you were strong enough for an hour minimum, but you didn't even tolerate it for ten minutes. They won't try it again until tomorrow, but it's a huge setback in getting you out of ICU. I've been asking you to squint your eyes if you're scared (i.e. when you're lucid—about 30 minutes a day) and you respond . . . don't be scared. I'm here and our love will get us through.

I love you.

Sal xxx

Vitals ♥	*11 am*		*9.40 pm*
BP:	127/46		149/60
Pulse:	67		70
CVP:	—		5
Temp:	37.4		—
O_2:	35%		35%
PEEP:	5 cm H_2O		5 cm H_2O
CPAP			CPAP

GCS:	9
Drugs	Antibiotics × 3
	Sodium
	Potassium

DAY 35: SUNDAY 21 MARCH 2010

Sammy, sleeper!

Young Samuel. Everyone is starting to get quite frustrated with you. You are not progressing from a PVS (persistent vegetative state) to 'waking up'. There seems to be little medical definition of the inbetween, so we (family) are calling it the MCS (minimally conscious state). You are worse today. You are not responding at all. No hand squeezes, no tongue poking, no stimulus to pain. Your GCS is awful, a 3. Life isn't worth living in this state, and we all know you would hate to exist as a 'vegetable'. You were successfully put on the TP for twenty minutes, which is great. I told you yesterday, you need to start tolerating it. Thing is, we just don't know what you're capable of. I know that you're in there, but to what degree? I just wish you'd make up your mind. I don't want you to suffer, so if you're not meant to be here, I want you to go. I know you wouldn't want to exist in this state. However, I know that you are capable of survival. The hardest part is getting you to 'awaken' because you're so strong you would fly through rehab, it's your personality. The process of 'waking' is slow, and could take weeks, months, years or not occur at all. I will not let you live out your days in a PVS in a nursing home with a nappy. No way.

Well, today you still haven't shown any signs of waking from the coma at all, which is disappointing. You should be responding with some degree of 'meaningfulness' by now, but you're just not. I'm at a loss; I just don't know what to do, expect, or prepare myself for. All I want is to have you back and live out all of our days together happily. Our life plan shouldn't have gone this way. It's now seven weeks from our wedding, which is extra hard. I'm not sure how it will be, on our 'wedding day'. Sitting in here with you, or being all alone because your time has ended; my wedding dress hanging in our wardrobe. I think I might be slightly depressed, but that is nothing compared to what you are going through. No matter what happens, I plan on wearing my engagement and wedding ring, always. I will also keep my chain around my neck, with your wedding ring on it, and St Christopher for strength and protection. Everyone is 'glum' today, trying to prepare me for the worst. They say you are slipping away. This isn't right. We knew from the first couple of weeks that we were destined to spend our lives together. I am not and will not accept that it won't happen. You are my soulmate, and I will never spend my life without you. How could I? You need to wake up. You

need to be OK. We need to spend our lives together, forever.
And it isn't your time!

I love you.

Sal xxx

Vitals	♥	11 am	
		BP:	143/54
		Pulse:	74
		GCS:	3
		O_2:	35%
		PEEP:	5 cm H_2O
		CPAP	
		20 minutes on TP (high-flow)	
Drugs		Cipro	
		Potassium	
		Sodium	

DAY 36: MONDAY 22 MARCH 2010

Sammy (G-unit)

Who has a lot of very, very loyal friends? Sammy G does.
Victor arrived from New York today! He spent the whole
day here supporting you and will also be back tomorrow.
It's amazing to watch how many people's lives you have
touched, Sam, it truly is. Everyone feels like you are their
best friend, and people I've never met are coming out of

the woodwork to see you. I'm not allowing them to see you though, because I know who you would and wouldn't want to have seen you in this state. Also if you haven't seen someone from 2006, I'm pretty sure you don't want them seeing you as you are! Annoying . . .

Anyhow, today has been relatively the same, all your vitals have been 'stable', with your GCS being between 3 and 8, depending on which hour we catch you.

Your sputum is getting thicker, stickier and yellower, so I know your infection's getting worse. You're on IV antibiotics for another five days, and then oral. Ventilation has been fantastic, you've managed a total of four hours on the TP (high-flow ventilator). A speech pathologist came to prepare you for the neuro ward, so that's promising. Now, you must control that infection! Oh! You burped!

As always, our love will get us through. I love you.

Sal xxx

Vitals   ♥   *9 pm*

BP:	154/68
Pulse:	76
Temp:	37.1
Resp Rate:	27
O_2:	30%
PEEP:	5 cm H_2O
CPAP	
4 hours on TP (high-flow)	

Drugs	Cipro
	Potassium
	Sodium

DAY 37: TUESDAY 23 MARCH 2010

Sammy superb!

Nothing is more reassuring and comforting to me than your magical kiss and today I have been blessed with superb kisses. Each time I have asked for one today you have puckered up more than usual, you handsome old romantic you! I love it that even though you don't appear to be 'awake', something is registering inside your mind . . . recognising me. It must be our souls, because I know our love has intertwined our souls, hearts and minds for an eternity. I can tell by listening to your slow, deep breaths, your heart rate is below 70, and your eyes are closed tight. There is no flickering behind the eyelids—your mind is peaceful, body relaxed, and every now and then your eyebrows move and your mouth moves as if you're in a relaxed dream. It's amazing. I love seeing you so calm. Today has been a big day. Josh and I wore you out early on by doing muscle-building exercises and Joshie gave you a 'rub-down'. Oh boy, did you hate it! You scrunched up your face as if you were annoyed: über-cute, if you ask me. Physio has been, you've had two baths (due to excessive sweating) and you were lying in an awkward position, so you got grouchy.

I love you.

Sal xxx

Vitals:	♥ 8.04 pm	
	BP:	142/59
	Pulse:	65
	Temp:	37.1
	Resp Rate:	23
	TP (high-flow) × 8 hours!	
Drugs	Cipro	
	Potassium	
	Sodium	

DAY 38: WEDNESDAY 24 MARCH 2010

Sleepy Sammy

Young Goddard—are you not ready to wake up yet? I'm ready. In fact, the whole world is ready to see your beautiful smiling face again. Eleven hours on TP/high-flow yesterday, all day and all night! One step closer to the ward! Busy day—sitting in chair, CT scan (head—no changes from last), 40-minute physio session, tilt-table, speech pathologist and TP/high-flow! Wow! Vic has come again and is staying on our couch tonight . . . nothing much else to report.

I love you, I feel so connected to you, soulmate, despite the circumstances.

I love you.

Sal xxx

DAY 39: THURSDAY 25 MARCH 2010

Pseudomona Sammy

Just when things were going smoothly and we thought you were looking tip-top . . . *grrr*. Turns out you have one very resistant pseudomona! You will always have them, that's a given, it's part of your CF. But, a resistant one? Please! We don't want or need it. You have been moved to bed 10, a secluded 'infection' room opposite your old bed 16. Bed 16 had one wall of windows, but only had curtains separating the cubicles. Bed 10 is four walls, one made of glass looking out onto the nurses' station. I guess it's a good move . . . it's quiet, you can play your music loud, but we can't hear the doctors when they do their rounds and it doesn't have good history. The last six weeks, I've only seen one patient make it 'out' of bed 10 to a ward, he was a 45-year-old leukaemia patient with two kids.

This room has negative energy. I have asked the spirits and energies to leave. Their negative energy isn't welcome here. Your mum is bringing in some crystals to cleanse the room. I've asked both our guides to protect us, shelter us, and to make sure this change in scenery is for a positive outcome. Good news is—if you go to a ward, you can go with the pseudomona! Yay! It also means you get your own room up there, instead of sharing with three others.

I love you, soulmate!

Sal xxx

Vitals	♥	3.20 pm	
		BP:	152/61
		Pulse:	78
		Resp Rate:	33
		GCS:	10
		TP (high-flow) from 5 am (aim to do this overnight too!)	
Drugs		Cipro	
		Potassium	
		Sodium	
		GCS:	8

DAY 41: SATURDAY 27 MARCH 2010

Sam is amazing

Darling, I'm so sorry I didn't write yesterday; nothing much happened! Tonight you are looking devilishly handsome as usual, the nurse has given you a lovely shave, and a great wash all over. Well, you certainly are amazing. At 4 this morning they changed your ventilation over to the 'low-flow' from the 'high-flow'. The low-flow is somewhat equivalent to only having an oxygen mask on your face, but because you have the trachea in, it goes on your stoma (where the trachea comes out of your neck). They also took out your central venous line, which means you are no longer reliant on drugs and are stable! Yay! Next up is going from the low-flow to the 'ward circuit', which means no assisted ventilation attached, you simply breathe from your trachea!

I love you.

Sal xxx

Vitals ♥

GCS:	9

DAY 42: SUNDAY 28 MARCH 2010

Sammy, Shambala warrior

I'm feeling really low and down today. I don't care what anyone says, no-one knows you like your partner. No-one. Not even our parents. They have each other to talk to, hug, sleep, visit, console—they have each other. I don't. My soulmate, my best friend, my lover, my everything, is lying in bed. Six long weeks without my other half. It's hard. I can talk to other people about what's going on, but it's not the same. It's not. You're the only one I want to talk to. You're my world, and I feel like nobody understands.

I love you.

Sal xxx (and Ralphie and Georgie)

Vitals ♥

GCS: 6

DAY 43: MONDAY 29 MARCH 2010

Super sleepy Sammy

Well, who is a grouch today?!?!? On the day when you're supposed to show off to the doctors you get grouchy and tired and refuse to show them your potential! Good one! Not your fault, though, you had a very sleepless night because the nurse gave you lots of turns, so you were being constantly moved. Then this morning the physio gave you a massive workout, the doctors all assessed you, they put you in the chair, and now you're about to be put on the tilt-table! Wow . . . no wonder you're grouchy.

You are sleeping now, which is good (albeit sitting upright)! Sleep is so very, very important with a head injury. As you can imagine, any tiny movement is exhausting. I keep telling you each time you rest, your mind and body is healing, and that each time you wake up, your mind will feel clearer and your body stronger. You're still not really opening your eyes, and that's not a good sign . . .

I love you.

Sal xxxx

Vitals   ❤

GCS: 10

DAY 44: TUESDAY 30 MARCH 2010

Sammy

What a huge day! You've finally moved to Ward 9B South, bed 20. After a massive morning you sat (assisted) on the side of the bed and helped support yourself. That is huge, and we are all so proud of you. The physios and family can see you improving, but the doctors can't, and they are the most important people to show it to. You're not responding at all to the doctors. Now we know why we're in Ward 9B South . . . they didn't know what to do with you, and they couldn't find a medical team to take you on. It's quite difficult to label you because you're not a straight neuro or respiratory case. So we have ended up under a random medical team in the general medical ward. A doctor came to consult us and said that basically we are here because you are not 'improving or responding' to doctors and DO

NOT QUALIFY FOR REHAB. Yes, as you can imagine that was like taking a semi-trailer to the heart. I don't give a shit what they say, I know you will be a medical mystery and *miracle*. The doctor said you will either die, or move to a nursing home. What BULLSHIT! Give it time, and I know you'll amaze them!

Our love will get us through.

I love you.

Sal xxx

DAY 45: WEDNESDAY 31 MARCH 2010

I am the master
> *Of my fate*
I am the captain
> *Of my soul*
—William Henley, 1875.
'Invictus'

I love you.

Sal xxx

DAY 46: THURSDAY 1 APRIL 2010

Sensitive Sammy

I upset you. I am so sorry. I read to you Rich's email, and when it said he was coming as a surprise to the wedding, you had the most pained expression on your face, and then you cried. Tears welled up in your eyes, falling down your face. But, I asked you if you wanted me to keep going and you gave me a big double eyebrow raise, so you can handle it . . . the doctors are still not seeing any progress, so I've started recording it to show them! You've also moved to Ward 8B North, Bed 41 now, under your 'home ward'—respiratory.

I love you.

Sal xxx

DAY 47: FRIDAY 2 APRIL 2010

Good . . . Friday!

It's getting hard, Sammy. Hard for everyone. We all know your recovery will take years, but we are all impatient people! I have a feeling it's going to be so slow that I won't hear your beautifully husky voice for around 8–10 months. Although you are progressing, it's slow. Super slow. You poked your tongue out today, which is a huge feat! You haven't done that for three weeks. Bad news is you have another infection. Good news is they caught it early and are treating it.

Overall, I'm so proud of you. I'm more in love with you than ever. Our love will conquer all.

I love you.

Sal xxx

DAY 48: SATURDAY 3 APRIL 2010

Easter Saturday

Certainly doesn't feel like Easter, Sammy. You're so smart and sharp, the speech therapist said it would take 5–7 days for you to learn to close your mouth . . . *two hours*! That's all it's taken. I'm so proud of you. You're a miracle, each and every day you fight you're a miracle. Today you've gotten a staph infection, another little setback, but nothing a broad spectrum antibiotic can't solve. I'm so in love with you it's not funny. You light a fire in my heart and soul that can never be put out. Our love will get us through. I love you.

Sal xxx

DAY 49: SUNDAY 4 APRIL 2010

Happy Easter!

Who's a smarty pants? Samuel Lawrence Goddard is! Only one day after testing positive for a staph infection, you and your vitals, along with your lungs and bloods, look great. It takes months for it to be out of your blood, but you're just improving with the antibiotics out of sight. They've made you sleepy but that's OK. Day 49 and I haven't missed one day of seeing you yet. The minimum hours I stay are eight, but usually I'm here twelve hours a day, all day, every day! And I love it. As long as I'm close to you I'm good. Day 49, or week seven, and I've finally been able to jump into bed and give you a proper hug. It felt amazing snuggling you, just like at home. Seven weeks and I only just did the first grocery shop! The dogs were having Daddy's Weetbix for brekky and tuna for dinner for a week 'cos I was all out. I'm too busy here to do any of that stuff.

Oh! Yesterday I put my cheek on yours for a cuddle and you moved your head to be closer to me. And today while you were sleeping you lifted my arm up to right angles! All this muscle work I'm doing with you is working . . . as always, our love will conquer all, I'm more in love than ever . . .

I love you.

Sal xxx

DAY 50: MONDAY 5 APRIL (I'M GOING CRAZY) 2010

Sam + Sal = love

I'm a little angry at the world today. Angry at the situation. I'm just ready to have you back, I guess. I want my lover, partner, soulmate, fiancé back. I know the longer you rest the better you're healing, but it's going on two months now without having our regular life together. Although something tells me nothing about our life will ever be 'regular' again. You have opened your eyes twice today, once briefly and the second time for 37 seconds, eye one-third open. I've also made a sign for your room so everyone can see it before coming in. It says . . .

STOP!
- ♥ *Wear a gown*
- ♥ *Wash hands well*

SMILE
- ♥ *Positive talk only*
- ♥ *NO CRYING and NO SAD FACES*
- ♥ *NO DISCUSSING WHAT HAPPENED or WHAT COULD*

LAUGH
- ♥ *But quiet voices only*
- ♥ *One conversation at a time*
- ♥ *NO PHONE CALLS—take it in the hall*
- ♥ *Phones on silent*

TALK TO SAM
- ♥ *Not at him*

This is to ensure you have only positive energy around you. I know you're hearing everything we say, in fact, it's funny because when you 'sleep' you respond with the best facial expressions. So I know you're at least taking it all in subliminally. Tomorrow I start part-time work. I don't want to leave you, but I can't lose my job, or we'll go bankrupt! So

I'll be working Tuesdays, Saturdays and Sunday mornings, 8 am til 12 pm and then I'll be straight back to nurse you back to health. Joshie will be here when I'm not for those few hours. You're usually sleeping then anyway.

I love you.

Sal xxx

DAY 51: TUESDAY 6 APRIL 2010

Shaking Sammy

Who is a clever bunny? You are! I just asked if you were tired and you squeezed your eyes 'yes'. I then asked if you were going to have a big sleep and you gently shook your head side to side! Yay! Today you had an ECG (echocardiogram), an ultrasound of your heart and I got to watch the whole thing. It was amazing! Even though you're not opening your eyes properly—or much at all—you're a lot more aware mentally. You also raised your arm twice for physio and once for blood pressure—without prompting! Amazing!

Your love keeps me strong.

I love you.

Sal xxx

DAY 53: THURSDAY 8 APRIL 2010

Soulmate

Today it's 30 days until our wedding. Even though I've postponed it—which, believe me, was a hard decision in itself, I'm looking forward to the day. I'm going to sleep over the night prior to the day so I can wake up with you and spend as much time as possible with you alone. Hmm, I've never quite understood the 'depth' of love, but now I do. Our bond is unbroken, unconquered by the challenges. It's become stronger and wiser and I know this is the type of unconditional love only ever felt once in a lifetime. My heart still flutters every time I kiss you and you kiss me back. It pounds when you do the slightest thing to show improvement and it soars when I look at you. I feel just as in love, if not more than the moment we met, the time spent under the shooting star, Mount Cootha, the airport when you returned from New York, the moment we got engaged, or our engagement party. It's unbelievable how much you realise the person lying in front of you really is your TRUE soulmate, in fact there's nothing quite like it.

Our love, true love, is like lighting a fire in your soul and it never going out, and I hope our love always makes you feel that way. I still kiss and cuddle you a million times a day. I promise to nurse you back to health with love. Our love is unbroken.

I love you.

Sal xxx

DAY 54: FRIDAY 9 APRIL 2010

Sammy, Shambala warrior!

I am always in awe of how amazing you are and how much you fight! The head of your medical team was so impressed with your improvements, if you continue like this by Monday, she will get the rehab doctor down to re-assess you and see if you're eligible for rehab. Yay! That's HUGE! You've also been taken off all antibiotics by the infectious diseases doctor and this morning you just randomly moved your arm over your torso without prompting! You also leaned forward for a kiss and kissed me on the cheeks. No eye opening today, though. You also had your first shower in almost eight weeks! You were just too fragile to move before now.

I love you, soulmate.

Sal xxx

DAY 55: SATURDAY 10 APRIL 2010

Super smiley Sammy

So we started the day out rough! I came in at 6.30 am to find you coughing up a lot of blood from your trachea . . . turns out your secretions have increased and too many suctions down your trachea caused trauma, but you seem all healed now. I went to work for four hours and now you're resting soundly. Funniest thing happened today! The physio let down your trachea cuff (which stops you from talking) when you coughed, so I heard your 'voice' for the first time in almost two *months*! HUGE! It was *awesome*! I was then pulling out a voice recording you had made of yourself, to show the physio what you sounded like . . . and when I played it you smiled! Joshie, Goldie and I burst into laughter, and you also 'laughed' and smiled!

It was amazing! We all laughed and smiled together for well over a minute and a half! Seriously, one of the biggest highs we have had in the last two months. I took a photo and of course video-recorded it for proof for the doctors. I sent the pic via SMS to all the family, so Luke sent back a voice message from Myles telling you how much he loves you, and to 'wake-up, Uncle Sam!' It was very cute! I asked you if you liked it and you squeezed my hand, so I ended up playing it over and over again 'cos you kept squeezing my hand. You truly are a miracle and you improve in leaps and bounds every day. Your love pulls me through.

I love you.

Sal xxx

DAY 58: TUESDAY 13 APRIL 2010

Scootin' Sammy

Another day! Big tilt-table session, which is great. Your ICU physio visited and is *very* impressed with your improvements.

Today I took you for your first excursion on the 'chair', around the ward. I sat you in front of the window overlooking Brisbane and you opened your eyes for approximately 80 seconds. You laughed at me 'cos I was trying to describe your poo's consistency to your mum—ha ha!

I'm falling more and more in love, each and every day . . .

Super-exhausted.

I love you.

Sal xxx

DAY 59: WEDNESDAY 14 APRIL 2010

Sometimes Sammy

Unsure how I feel today. The most difficult part of each day is, always, going to bed. Time after time I try to go to bed, only to find it all very lonely once again. I find myself sitting in bed hours and hours after I intended to go to sleep, doing anything possible to distract me from the very real, raw and emotional fact that you, my one, only, true, soulmate is not there . . . Hmm. Ouch. It hurts an unbelievable amount. All those pesky nights I spent angry at you for not cuddling me, I should have just appreciated the fact I was lucky enough to be lying next to you. You are one truly amazing, remarkable soul. I've always known this. My love for you has always been intense, however, now it has manifested into an obsession to protect you, shield you and guide you.

I feel like I've got a newborn baby and I don't want to let it out of my sights for even one second. That's how precious and fragile you are to me. I feel a bit torn, really, when I get home at night. I'm feeling a mixture of exhaustion, sadness and anger (that this has happened to you and not me) . . . you have so much more to give to the world, so much more life than me. You gave me life, when we fell in love, you lit a spark, a fire in my soul. You brought me to life. All I can think is that you were chosen because you are strong enough and equipped with the right tools to survive this. I'm not as strong as you. All my love and energies are focused solely around you. You are my world. Life will never be the same again and there are so many 'what ifs'—but as long as you want me, I'm ready to start a new life with you. You have the love I need to see me through. It's real. Our love, Chapters 1 (dating), 2 (engaged), and 3 (post injury) have all survived to date through our love. There's no doubt. Progression-wise, lots of thumbs-up/thumbs-down today. Forty-five minutes on the tilt-table (yay!) and the doctor put in a rehab referral. Speech therapy needs you to swallow a *lot* more! Then the speech valve goes in so we can hear your voice, woo hoo!

I love you.

Sal xxx

DAY 60: THURSDAY 15 APRIL 2010

The unexpected Sammy

Big day today. Your second shower in almost nine weeks, and I gave it to you. Yay! You also brought your legs together for the first time while sitting in your chair, knees together—all was *awesome*! Tonight you were sleeping soundly (pulse at 56) when all of a sudden you 'woke up,' eyes half open, lifting your chest halfway off the bed, legs and arms moving. All one fluid motion. Then, within seconds, asleep again. Almost 40 full minutes of off-on eye-opening today— awesome! And we also electrically stimulated your jaw to strengthen the muscles for swallowing.

I love you.

Sal xxx

DAY 62: SATURDAY 17 APRIL 2010

Silly Sammy + Sal

Sorry I didn't write yesterday, Sammy, after eight weeks and six days, it's fair to say I'm physically, mentally and emotionally exhausted. I went home after eleven hours by your bedside and slept, slept, slept. I tell ya, I'm not much of a friend, daughter, sister . . . or anything these days. Outside of the hospital, outside of 'Stroke World'—I literally have no idea what's going on. Don't ask me what is on the news or what's going on in a friend's world—'cos I don't know!

I honestly spend so much time inside the hospital I don't know what the weather is like. Honest! Yesterday and today you opened your eyes on and off for over 40 minutes. Yay! The footy was on tonight so you listened and 'watched' your favourite team win!

I love you.

Sal xxx

DAY 63: SUNDAY 18 APRIL 2010

Spak-attack, Sal!

Well, didn't you just think it was hilarious today when I had a hissy fit to the nurses over your care? You laughed at me. Ha ha! Well, when they forget numerous times to connect the air to your trachea, it's just not on! You cannot breathe without air! As you can't talk I have to speak on your behalf. Hmm, anyways . . . you're opening your eyes more but are now emotionally processing what's happened and that's really difficult to watch. All we can do is love and support you while you go through the emotions. I know we have a long two-year rehab haul ahead of us, but I'm just hanging out to hear 'I love you'—or feel you hug me . . . I love you.

Sal xxx

DAY 64: MONDAY 19 APRIL 2010

Sick Sammy

Ugh! What a day. You're crook again . . . you're on three antibiotics now, for a chest infection and a suspected bladder/bacterial infection from your catheter. It was dirty and blocked (with over one litre of urine stuck in your bladder) so they put two in with no luck. Now you have a hard plastic condom on your willy which drains through a bag into a tube. HIGHLIGHT . . . you lifted up both legs today, which is enormous! You did it lots 'cos you were in pain but now you realise you can do it, it's a huge recovery step! Previously we hadn't really seen much/any (independent) leg movement so this is wonderful. I'm ridiculously in love with you today.

I love you!

Sal xxx

DAY 65: TUESDAY 20 APRIL 2010

Supercalifragilisticexpealidocious

You poor thing my honey-pie! It hurt so much when you peed tonight that your face was all scrunched up, you were obviously in excruciating pain, so they gave you some morphine-based pain killers. Well, you looked instantly peaceful once you felt it kick in.

You let me lie all snuggled up in bed with you for 45 minutes—the best time I've had in 65 days . . . actually being able to hold you really tight. The sweetest thing was you turning your head to touch mine and puckering up for a kiss . . . it set my heart alight. I'm more in love with you than ever.

I love you.

Sal xxx

DAY 66: WEDNESDAY 21 APRIL 2010

Sammy Superstar!

Arm above head-stretch. Tick. Leg up-stretch out. Tick. AMAZING! The physio said seeing you do these two huge things made her day, and all the medical staff (and us, of course) are elated. The doctor has asked the rehab doctor to come next week to assess you, to ensure you get the best possible shot at rehab. There is even talk of starting you with semi-solids in your mouth next week—that's how strong your swallow is—one step closer to the trachea out! Eyes still aren't opening much but your kiss is stronger . . . feels magical when you kiss me back . . . pure magic.

I love you.

Sal xxx

DAY 67: THURSDAY 22 APRIL 2010

Superhuman Sam!

Who's a clever cookie? You! Today you learnt how to push and pull with your arms and boy did you give me a mighty push! Ha ha! Everyone (physios and nurses) was very impressed. I guess you really are sick of hearing my voice for twelve hours a day! I also smothered you with kisses and you laughed and smiled . . . mmm . . . I love kissing you! Your poo doesn't look quite right so it's being sent off for testing, you might have a tummy ache. The rehab referral is in which is massive, so it's all upwards and onwards from here!

I love you.

Sal xxx

DAY 68: FRIDAY 23 APRIL 2010

Amanda's 27th Birthday

Today was hectic! I got called in to work at the last minute, which meant I was in such a hurry that I didn't get to see you until 12.30 pm today! Urgh! Very unusual for me, 'cos on the days I usually work I always come at 6.30 am to see you before work. Anyway . . . now I'm working two full nine-hour days a week starting tomorrow. Will be super hard. Today was Mandy's birthday and all she wanted was to celebrate and open her pressies with you in hospital. It was really nice.

I love you, always and forever . . . You leave me speechless.

Sal xxx

DAY 69: SATURDAY 24 APRIL 2010

Super snuggly Sammy!

My first full day of work today was agony. If only we were
millionaires and I could stop work, still pay the bills and
spend every waking moment with you. Tonight I (as usual)
overly smothered you with hugs! You laughed and smiled,
awesome! You also gave me my first proper hug—with
downward pressure on my back as not to let go—a hard
move! You also did your first high-five, and I think you were
so pleased with yourself, as you kept on doing it! I filled
out the rehab referral form. Yay! The wheels are in motion.

I love you.

Sal xxx

DAY 70: MONDAY 26 APRIL 2010

Yup, I love ya, Sam

Another day of falling head over heels in love with you . . .
who is lucky enough to be falling in love with their soulmate twice? Me! I have all those kooky feelings of blissful
love—like when we started dating, all over again! And I
love it! Today I got to put the uridone on you (it's like a

condom with a bag and tube connected, for your pee)—very interesting first time! Ha ha! I also accidentally stuck my hand in your poo—ha ha! Was funny. Sorry I didn't write yesterday . . . two full days of work knackered me, so I went straight to sleep. We are seeing lots more emotions from you which is great . . . not much in the eyes though.

I love you.

Sal xxx

DAY 72: TUESDAY 27 APRIL 2010

Madopar Sammy

So, you're on Madopar now, which is a Parkinson's Disease drug to stop the shaking in your arms. It isn't really working, but it's making you super-drowsy and you're not partici-pating in physio 'cos you're zonked. Hopefully they stop it soon! Today you did ten swallows in a row and answered all of the speech therapist's questions correctly, so they are going to start you on jelly! Yay! It's one HUGE step towards getting that trachea out! Amazing. I love you so super-incredibly much. Mwah, mwah, mwah!

Sal xxx

DAY 73: WEDNESDAY 28 APRIL 2010

Speechless Sammy

Wow, huge day today! I'll start with the rehab—the doctors came and did their first assessment, and to be honest, they weren't too interested. They said you need to be 'medically stable' i.e.: no trachea, no ongoing chest problems, normal sleep and wake (eyes open) cycles, eating solid food. We are months away from achieving any of those, *but*, good news is they will assess you every Wednesday to see how you're progressing! Bad news is . . . it's a 26-bed unit for Queensland and half of New South Wales! One big, big, big milestone for today was with the speech team. They let down your trachea cuff for fifteen minutes and you said 'Argh!' I cried. It felt amazing to hear your voice.

I love you.

Sal xxx

DAY 74: THURSDAY 29 APRIL 2010

Rich, Sam + Sal

What a lovely day today. Cliff, Tik and Melissa (who was next to you in ICU) came to visit—Melissa was released from rehab today. Pete and Jules also visited from Woodford and Rich arrived, gallivanting in the middle of his world trip. I didn't get any alone time with you today—none. All I wanted to do was snuggle you tight, but that's a bit tough with so many visitors! The *amazing* nurse reckons you said 'Hey' last night when she was chatting to you! The speech therapist let down your trachea cuff again today and is so impressed with your strong 'Argh!' I can't wait til this trachea is out and you can get stronger! I love you so much.

Sal xxx

DAY 75: FRIDAY 30 APRIL 2010

Speakin' Sammy!

Huge day, handsome! Tilt-table, bed physio, sitting on the side of the bed, ball work (pushing and kicking ball), big OT session, 2 × chest physio sessions and 40 minutes with your speech valve on. You did tremendously well and the speech team is so surprised how loud and clear your voice is. I could see your frustration at not being able to form words yet, but the vocal cords are tired from not being used—I'm sure in a few weeks we won't be able to keep you quiet! Rich visited again today, I think he's off to Perth tomorrow, but he loved seeing you. Ralph and Georgie miss you so much and I really can't wait to see what you have in store for us next!

I LOVE YOU!

MWAH xxx

DAY 76: SATURDAY 1 MAY 2010

Hens and bucks

Tonight should have been our buck's and hen's nights . . .
at least I got to spend it with you, watching/listening to
the Reds v Brumbies games. I loved every second of it.
Today I realised I am operating as a robot would . . . I am
actually void of feeling anything emotional for other people.
I know why people in these situations become addicts to
drugs/booze—it's not to numb the pain, it's to actually feel
something real. I'm feeling really numb . . . but, I love you
more than the world.

Sal xxx

DAY 78: MONDAY 3 MAY 2010

VRE positive

Darling-heart. You've tested positive to VRE, which is a
hospital superbug. Apologies for not writing yesterday. I was
buggered emotionally and physically. Today we spent twelve
hours together and I loved it (this is the usual length of
time I stay with you—8 am to 8 pm). You loved it too—we
shared a BIG hug and you really loved it—you wouldn't let
go. Matty, Sharpie, Cal, Antonio and Goldie visited you
today, which was lovely. There is an amazing amount of love
and support around you, honey, I don't think you will ever

really understand how truly wonderful everyone has been for and to us both. As always, I love you more than ever.

Mwah. xxx

DAY 79: TUESDAY 4 MAY 2010

Sal and Sam: sad

Feeling a little useless and depressed today. I spent one and a half hours trying to calm you down and get you to sleep tonight, which of course I *do not mind at all*, but to be honest it is very emotionally and physically draining. All you wanted was for me to hold you tight, which I love! But after being at the hospital for eleven hours, and looking after you non-stop, not having a break myself, I felt totally and utterly useless, like there is nothing I can do to take your emotional pain away. The only thing that soothed you? A teddy to hold really tight and plenty of hugs and kisses from me, and pure exhaustion. I totally get your pain and frustration, I just wish I could take it all away for you.

I love you.

Sal xxx

DAY 80: WEDNESDAY 5 MAY 2010

Amazing Sammy

Almost three months in and we had our first hug standing up. You were on the tilt-table and I stole a quick moment to hug you and you put your arms around me (*without* any prompting)—it was simply AMAZING!

Today the doctor increased your Madopar dosage and it has knocked you for six—your pulse is high but you've slept almost the entire day. Speech valve went on again today and you said 'Argh' and 'Mmm' but we had to annoy you to get anything. You're still making progress—slowly but surely. I just can't wait to see what you do next—you miracle man. Today you made my heart flutter with love . . .

Sal xxx

DAY 81: THURSDAY 6 MAY 2010

Exhaustion—Sam + Sal

After three weeks of spending 1½–2 hours a night trying to calm and soothe your emotional 'ghoulies', I broke down. I always make a point *not* to show fear, negativity, sadness or weakness in front of you, but I actually got so frustrated I cried. There was *nothing* tonight that I could do to console you and after twelve hours looking after you, it's exhausting and frustrating. Sometimes I feel like nothing I do is helping you, and I feel so helpless for you—you can't *really* tell me how you're feeling. I'm emotionally dead. I can only love you.

I love you.

Sal xxx

DAY 82: FRIDAY 7 MAY 2010

The night before

I'm looking at this blank page and I'm not sure what to write. I feel somewhere beyond numb and intense pain. I can't quite describe it. I guess from tomorrow I'm 'a little bit married' so I'll be wearing my wedding ring on my left hand as a tribute to you. I don't know why, but this just feels like the right, natural thing to do. Dan and Lucie visited you today. Would have been amazing to have met them in better circumstances . . . I'm wondering if I'm what they call a 'smiling depressive'. I certainly feel depressed. Going to bed staring at my wedding dress hanging in the closet, wanting you back from the black hole you've fallen into. It just isn't fair.

I love you.

Sal xxx

DAY 83: SATURDAY 8 MAY 2010

Our wedding day

Today, Goddard, was meant to be our wedding day. Sigh. It will come, at some point or another—and what a magical day it will be. The nurses have been wonderful today. They organised for you to go outside!!

That's the first time since February 14, at 3 pm, that you've been outside. You opened your eyes and smiled. On a slightly bad note—you're back on antibiotics after a night of many secretions. But that too will pass. It's remarkable to watch your progress—even if it is at a snail's pace, you're progressing in leaps and bounds from every previous day. Still, I'm waiting for the day you say hello. I have a feeling it is months away.

Happy Wedding Day, husband.

I love you.

Sal xxx

DAY 84: SUNDAY 9 MAY 2010

A 'little bit married'

Today sucked. I'm now classifying myself as 'a little bit married', because, well, mentally I feel I did marry you yesterday. You have a chest infection so you're feverish, tired, grumpy. Tonight I watched 'Marley and Me' . . . I cried a lot. Sometimes (a lot) I feel compelled to do/watch/see things we did together (like watch 'Marley and Me')—it kind of gives me a real emotion, rather than just going through the robotic motions of day-to-day. It's Mother's Day. So I went to Mum's for lunch. Everyone was up from Adelaide (for our wedding) and wanting to 'talk' about how I feel/am coping. It's like having a crucifix. I'm feeling detached and depressed. Why us? It's all bullshit.

I love you.

Sal xxx

DAY 85: MONDAY 10 MAY 2010

Brothel and morgue

Two distinctly bonkers things happened to me today. First up, I was so terribly ill with tummy pain I thought I'd leave you for an hour and go and get a massage. It looked a tad cheap and when the girl took me into the room, the dirtiest, skankiest Thai 'lady-boy' was waiting for me! I freaked out, asked where the toilet was, and ran out of the back door! Can you imagine me running down the back alley?! Ha ha! What a sight to see! I've never felt so wrong in my life! Note to self: that massage parlour is really a brothel! Don't go!

The second bonkers thing was totally bizarre, you'll think I'm a nutjob. On my way home tonight, I thought I'd take a sneak peek at level 2, hydrotherapy pool and physio gym, where you'll be going (hopefully next month). As I'm walking down the hall I felt like a thousand people were pulling and grabbing at me, and I got the strongest words in my head 'you're not welcome here'. I kept going, then stopped, feeling overwhelmed. I looked up, only to see the sign 'mortuary' with an arrow pointing to two big doors at the end of the hall. Needless to say, I left! Not a good place for the 'hypersensitive' such as me. Was very, very creepy!

You're still crook today, poor bunny. I told you I had to work tomorrow and you cried. If only I didn't have to work. I love you more than ever and wish I was with you 24/7.

Sal xxx

DAY 86: TUESDAY 11 MAY 2010

Rain, rain, go away!

What a bugger of a day! It rained all day and wasn't very pleasant. You are still sick—a staph infection in your lungs, which isn't good. You had a fairly restful day, not doing much. After your little speech-valve shock yesterday (you panicked) you didn't tolerate it today. Improvement is slow but you are progressing. I snuck into bed with you for a good hour tonight—it was blissful!

Wondering how I'm going to cope going back to work full-time in July—I'm just not ready.

I love you × a billion.
Mwah! xxx

DAY 88: THURSDAY 13 MAY 2010

Ghoulies!

Sorry, I didn't write yesterday . . . I'm literally exhausted from spending twelve + hours a day here. You're having 'ghoulies' aka, you're anxious, upset etc. and nothing I do calms you. It's now 10 pm and I've been here since 8 am. You've been having ghoulies for almost four hours now. The dogs have been locked outside all this time, cold and hungry. How on earth can I get any sleep at night knowing you're like this? I can't leave til you're asleep, but I'm running myself dead. You got moved to the Infectious Diseases, ward today because you're colonised with VRE (superbug).

I don't know what to do. ARGH!

I'm at the end of my tether—I wish you'd relax!

Sal xxx

DAY 89: FRIDAY 14 MAY 2010

Three months

Today it's been three months since you were admitted to hospital. Wow, how time flies! I haven't worked full-time in three months! Crazy! Today you got to sit outside for the first time in three months! And for over an hour. You even got a faint tan. Your new room in Infectious Diseases is wonderful. It's new, big, clean, bright and it's Hector's (Kryssy's stepdad) old room!

The nurse who is on tonight seems to think you might have your trachea out early June, which would be amazing! Today you also chewed for the first time—a chico lolly wrapped in gauze. Well, I love you so much I'm dreading working tomorrow! I hate leaving you!

I love you, handsome.

Sal xxx

DAY 90: SATURDAY 15 MAY 2010

Love, love, love!

Hello, my name is Sally and I am a smotherer. I can't help it, especially when my Sammy G looks so deliciously handsome! I had to work today (bummer!) but I made you a board to point at when I ask you questions.

Oh! We officially have neighbours! They moved in today. I can't see much except one guy in the second bedroom and they have hideous taste in furniture! Mmm, I love you! LOTS!

Sal xxx

DAY 91: SUNDAY 16 MAY 2010

Lover, lover

When I look into your eyes all I feel is love. It's like the stars all fell from the sky and landed in your eyes. Every time I feel your touch I crumple at the knees, and when you kiss me sweetly all I do is smile—I appreciate it all—every single movement, every kiss, every touch, every smile, every tear, every fleeting moment I have with you. Not a second goes by that I don't feel admiration, praise and joy for you. You truly are my soulmate, my one and only, my one true love. I will marry you and it will be the greatest moment in our lives.

I love you, soulmate.

Sal xxx

DAY 92: MONDAY 17 MAY 2010

Tone

Hello, handsome. Today was an OK day—unfortunately the 'tone' in all of your muscles has stiffened a lot over the weekend. Not good. Your right leg has quite a significant 'drop' to it, which hurts to stretch and doesn't go flat (to stand). The physios and neurologists are thinking of putting Botox in your muscles to help. You've also been started on antidepressants, which take a few weeks to kick in. It's super-important though . . . depression is a huge after-effect of stroke. It sucks, but I'm here for you all of the way, so here's to hoping they work!

I love you.

Mwah!

Sal xxx

DAY 95: TUESDAY 18 MAY 2010

OMG, OMG, OMG!

You cheeky little shit! I was just sitting by your bed (I don't think you knew I was there!) and all of a sudden you just started doing all of these movements! It was *amazing*! I managed to get all of them on video and I can't wait to show the physio tomorrow—she will be blown away! It is such a tremendous feat—and you did it all with such ease and breeze. If you keep going this way, you'll be in rehab in no time. Maybe it's 'cos I got stuck into you today and told you if you didn't pull your shit together you'd end up in a nursing home. Tough love, but I had to shock you into it.

I LOVE you!

Mwah! Xxx

DAY 96: THURSDAY 20 MAY 2010

No money sucks ass

We are broke! Well, you've indicated lately you're sick of me (lots of angry yelling *at* me) so I am giving you a break Friday and Saturday nights. I guess three months of me twelve hours a day every day is enough . . . it hurts though . . .

I'm only trying to help. I love you.

Sal xxx

DAY 97: SATURDAY 22 MAY 2010

Lost my shit

My name is Sal, I'm 23, my fiancé is seriously ill and I have depression. This is Sal 2.0. Lost. Last night was Adam's birthday drinks. I went to fill the void of you not being there. I got drunk. Went home. You weren't there and I lost my shit. Like Britney-style total mental breakdown. I'm talking batshit crazy. I've never cried so hard and I just couldn't stop. I think I mourned our life that is gone now. Our neighbours found me on the kitchen floor. I haven't been able to function today. I just can't do anything. I didn't go to work, to see you, nothing. I'm paralysed with fear. What will happen to us? I *need* you to be OK.

Sal xxx

DAY 98: SUNDAY 23 MAY 2010

I'm aching for you

Today I put on a brave face and faced the world. I went to work, to see you. Your antidepressants have hit, and hard. You look drugged out of your brain. I got no emotion from you today, there was no light in your soul. I miss you. I miss us. I miss everything that our life used to be. I'm going to have to go back to work three days a week from next week, then full-time in July. I won't be able to pay all of our bills soon and I don't want to touch our savings. How will I manage being away from you? All I want to do is look after you 24/7. Would you have done this for me? Three months off work to care for me?

I LOVE YOU TOO MUCH.

Sal xxx

DAY 99: MONDAY 24 MAY 2010

AMAZING!

You are simply amazing! Today you did *21* leg raises in a row on your right leg! That's massive! We had a great day today, full of love together. I smothered you a little bit (a lot!)—sorry. I can't help it. I'm so in love with you sometimes the only way I can feel better is when I'm holding and hugging you. I need love sometimes too . . . I can only go a certain time without it. Tomorrow you get your PEG (feeding tube) in. It's a direct line into your tummy as it will be a few months until you eat again. I love, love, love you.

You're my soulmate.

I LOVE YOU!

Sal xxx

Chapter 3

New beginnings,
Rekindled love,
Sam, Invictus

❤

DAY 100: TUESDAY 25 MAY 2010

Bike pedals, tracheas and PEGS!

Hello, handsome! Today was an epic day! We started with physio, in which you did very, very well, tolerating standing on the tilt-table . . . however, you also used the bike pedals (with your hands) for the very first time! It was amazing. Your whole medical team was talking about it all day! Next up you had a new trachea put in as your old one was getting grotty. This one is now your third in 55 days! Huge! Thirdly you had the 'PEG' put in . . . it's a 20 cm tube × 20 mm (width) put surgically into your tummy. It's a long-term version of the nasal gastric (NG) tube. Although it's an indicator you won't be eating for a few months, at least the meds won't block the tube! I'm as in love with you as ever, and we shared a gorgeous 40-minute hug this morning . . . heaven.

Sal xxx

DAY 101: WEDNESDAY 26 MAY 2010

Bike pedals and wheelchairs

Dear Sammy. Handsome, handsome, Sammy. Another big day today! First off you 'pedalled' using the bike pedals, (whilst lying in bed), for ten minutes *independently*, forward and in reverse! Although slow, you did it!

Secondly, I snuck 500 ml of Ice Break (an iced-coffee drink) into your PEG! Haha! You loved it! Thirdly, this afternoon you moved your wheelchair three metres by yourself! Again, slowly, but all by yourself! Fourthly, it's State of Origin (game 1) tonight, so Matty, Houlty, Sharpie, Goldie and Antonio watched it with you. What great mates! Fifthly, I went to the doctors and they said I am missing bone in my jaw! *Eek*! From that scuba diving accident! No wonder I'm in pain! Sixthly, I am more in love with you than ever!

I love you!

Sal xxx

DAY 102: THURSDAY 27 MAY 2010

Work, red switches, love

Hello soulmate! Well, another epic day! I had to go to work and had to commit to working full-time July to January. UGH! I wish I could stay part-time until you're better. You had casts taken today of your legs using plaster of Paris to make customised splints (lucky boy!). This will help your 'drop-foot'. The physio gave you a giant red switch/button for you to press with your foot for attention. Eventually it'll be attached to the nurse/call button. I asked you to answer my equations by pressing the switch (eg. $10-7=??$) and you answered them all perfectly! You're still as switched on as ever! I can't wait until you're fully recovered to take you back here and show all of those non-believers! Mmm, I love you immensely.

I love you.

Sal xxx

DAY 103: FRIDAY 28 MAY 2010

Mmm, Sam!

Hello, handsome! Mmm, I love you × you're super-delicious and I had an amazingly wonderful day today! We had so many great hugs (totally invaluable) and you pedalled the bike pedals for so long and super fast! It was incredible to watch! What else happened . . . you looked super-gorgeous when I put your beanie and jumper on to go outside in the cold to watch the sunset . . . holding hands (super-romantic!). Pretty much I'm just amazingly, super, romantically in love with you and am savouring every imaginable time with you possible before I go back to full-time work. I love kissing you.

I love you.

Sal xxx

DAY 104: SATURDAY 29 MAY 2010

Joshie's birthday

Hello deliciously-handsome husband-to-be! Well, today is Joshie's 32nd birthday and he got to see you for the first time in four weeks! He has been in Sydney working, but can see a huge improvement in you in that time. I had to work today, which sucks! But it does mean that when I see you after work I over-smother you and you laugh at me! I love getting a smile and a giggle out of you, no matter how small it is!

Ralph and Georgie say hello and 'we love you, Daddy'. They still think you're coming in the door any minute and Ralph listens out for your car.

I love you, mwah.

Sal xxx

DAY 106: MONDAY 31 MAY 2010

Lover, lover, superstar!

Dear lover, oh my, what a superstar you are! This morning after I showered you, you put your very own deodorant on! Yay! That's a huge unassisted first! You also leant forward on your own initiative for me to dry your back and put your shirt on. Wow—it's simply amazing watching your progress. I'm in awe of you.

There is no-one on this planet, or in this lifetime as strong-willed and persistent as you, my love. I'm feeling seriously overwhelmed with love! We had two big 15-minute hugs today—and it was bliss. Nothing makes me feel better than a hug from you, my one and only.

Ever thine, ever mine, ever ours.

I love you!

Sal xxx

DAY 108: WEDNESDAY 2 JUNE 2010

The smell of dying lungs

Urgh! Another super-busy day. Sorry I didn't write yesterday my lover-lover, I've been superbly exhausted. I think the stress of worrying about going back to work full time, your care and finances have done it.

On another note—the lady in Bed 8 next to you is having stem cell treatment for advanced cancer. The smell is beyond horrendous. I actually almost fainted from the smell alone today. It smelt like what I would imagine a decaying body to smell like. It's the smell of her lungs dying apparently—and the smell will last five days!

You had a bumper day today with eleven people in your room at once! Speechies, occupational therapists, physios, chest physios, nurses and me! Whoa! You're pooped now. Another sleep and we start all over again. I love you, soulmate!

Sal xxx

DAY 109: THURSDAY 3 JUNE 2010

Gym!

Darling! Great news! You have been given permission by your doctors to go to the physios' very new, high-tech gym *every* day! This is massive! Yay! We had a good day today. I'm so buggered I've come home to crash. Almost four months of 10–12 hour days with only one day off so far, not to mention the physical, emotional and financial stress and strain—I guess that will do it to you! Anyway, I shouldn't complain—look at you, simply amazing. I'm just grateful I still have you. I love you more than ever!

All my eternal love . . .

I love you, soulmate.

Sal xxx

DAY 110: FRIDAY 4 JUNE 2010

Mmm, delicious!

Hello, handsome! Well didn't you look delicious today? It was an epic day—usually you get 2–3 hours' sleep during the day . . . today you got fifteen minutes!

We had some amazing hugs. I had you sitting on the edge of the bed and I was supporting you. Your head was nuzzled in my boobs with your arms wrapped around me—should have seen your face! Ha ha! Utter contentment. It was your first gym day—fifteen minutes on the bike and you stood up (assisted) three times! HUGE!

So very, very exciting. There is talk of your trachea coming out in three weeks. Yay! So exciting.

Ever thine, ever mine, ever ours.

Sal xxx

DAY 112: SUNDAY 6 JUNE 2010

Do, re, mi

Hello, hunky husband-to-be! Hmmmm . . . another delightful weekend at work. (Ha ha!) Gosh, I hate being away from you—I'm sure you love the break! Ha!

I couldn't stop singing 'Do re mi, so fa la ti' etc. today but couldn't figure out why. I got to the hospital and your mum was singing it to you! Wow—creepy, huh?!

You've had a super-sleepy weekend—I think the Friday gym session took it out of you. Your cuff has been down 10 hours today—huge! A good sign the trachea should come out in around a month!

I love you!

Mwah!

Sal xxx

DAY 113: MONDAY 7 JUNE 2010

Handsome

You looked so delicious today! I washed all of your shirts but brought in a different set today to give you a bit of variety! I think I brought in about . . . mmm . . . maybe 25 shirts! I have this rule that you must be showered, shaved, teeth brushed, deodorant on, and in your own clothes every single morning! It takes me about one hour at the moment to do all of that to you—it's no mean feat! Today I put you in a shirt I don't recall seeing before so it must have been new and you look handsome. We sat in the sun all morning and you went brown. Pale ale old me, I went red. Ha ha! I'm hanging out to see you again tomorrow—I can't wait. Ever thine, ever mine, ever ours.

I love you.

Sal xxx

DAY 114: TUESDAY 8 JUNE 2010

Reaching out

Hey Sammy, I'm baffled. Google as much as you want and you won't find *any* stories from a stroke survivor about what they went through. Nothing! No inspirational stories, no words of wisdom and no hope, no guidance. This just spurred me on even more to write a book. There is heaps of stuff *about* stroke survivors—and so there should be, but why not about how it's affected the carer/partner and certainly not in our age group! I'm going to do this for us and to help others, to show them it is OK to talk about it, and it is OK to crumble into a million pieces. I can't repair you, I can only love you. And I love you more than ever.

Sal xxx

DAY 115: WEDNESDAY 9 JUNE 2010

I can walk and stand

Hey lover-lover. What a glorious day together today. Barely any 'ghoulies' and I gave you a whole Ice Break down your PEG and some in your mouth too. You loved it.

In gym today you stood up with the help of the physios and I moved your legs to simulate walking. I imagine in a year or so you'll be running and I won't be able to catch you! Last night I started writing the book. It felt so good. I started with our love stories and it reminded me of all the things you used to do. Leaving roses under my windscreen wiper so I'd find them once I got off the train from work. I really hope our love is the same after all of this. I'm scared you won't love me.

I love you.

Sal xxx

DAY 117: FRIDAY 11 JUNE 2010

Don't blame me

Hello, handsome. Well today would've been my nanna's birthday. It's my first 11 June since Nanna's been gone. I've thought of her today . . . you had some 'ghoulies' so I smothered you and said in a funny voice—'Don't hate me, don't blame me, it's not my fault, you're just so delicious. Mmm I might have to eat you.' And I had a million giggles! So I'll have to keep doing it! You're getting so much stronger with your standing transfers from bed to chair and vice versa. No more sling and hoist! I love, love, love, love you! You'll rocket ahead in no time and it'll be our wedding.

I love you.

Mwah!

Sal xxx

DAY 119: SUNDAY 13 JUNE 2010

SATC2

It's 11.52 pm on the night before my 24th birthday. I'm sitting alone in our bed thinking . . . not good. The girls took me to see 'Sex and the City 2'. I *hated* being away from you, watching women in the movie have all the things I'll possibly never have . . . a marriage and kids to the man I love. Every single day I wonder what the future holds. Will you love me, want me, care for me, need me? It's a very real possibility that after this you'll change and not want a relationship with me. You may grow to hate me when our loving 'husband–wife' relationship becomes 'patient–carer' . . . I'm unbelievably scared you won't want me. What happens then?

DAY 120: MONDAY 14 JUNE 2010

24 + 60

Howdy handsome husband!

Today is your dad and my birthdays! (Yay—sarcastically!) You and I spent the entire day together and then at 4 pm the whole crew came to the hospital for cake time. Lots of pressies—you gave me a new perfume which I bought and had giftwrapped! Ha ha! You also got me Lindt choccies and a card which Manda organised. We got your Dad the 60-year State of Origin book. ALSO: today you took EIGHT assisted steps! That's massive! The wardie was doing a standing transfer with you from chair to bed and you just put one foot in front of the other and so on and so on!

AMAZING!

I love you!

DAY 121: TUESDAY 15 JUNE 2010

Cast me away

Darling! Well today was a big day! It's been five days since you had Botox in your arms and leg, so after physio, they 'serial casted' your right leg. This is awesome, because it'll help your 'drop foot' correct, and will in turn allow you to put more weight on that leg. This will increase standing and walking ability. It took one hour to cast your foot and on Friday they'll saw it off and put another one on . . . and so on and so on until your foot's at a 45-degree angle. They made it blue 'cos they all know you're a NSW fan! Ritch and Kate came in and so did Luke and Josh. I let you have some brotherly time. I love you more than anything.

You're my all, soulmate.

Mwah!

Sal xxx

DAY 123: THURSDAY 17 JUNE 2010

Drains and dishwashers

Howdy, handsome! Well, you'll be 'happy' to know that since you've gone into hospital, stress has done all sorts of weird things to me! I now have to dye my hair super-blonde to cover the greys. I have adult acne—I never had a pimple when growing up! I've got wrinkles galore and I'm fat-as considering I barely eat! Tonight Adam, Sym and I spent the third week in a row trying to fix the dishwasher drains—there is an epic blockage somewhere. I also got a doggy house for the boys and, best of all, I spent eleven hours with you, snuggling and taking care of you! Mmm, so incredibly in love.

Marry me.

Mwah!

Sal xxx

DAY 124: FRIDAY 18 JUNE 2010

Well superlover-lover, you really don't realise just how hard it is to do this all without you. It's strange, we have both been through so much and it will bond us, but you'll never really realise what I've gone through and vice versa. It's like someone has died, because life as we knew it will never be the same. And no matter how much we think otherwise, we have changed and will never be the same again individually, or as a couple. I miss everything while embracing our new and existing life. I want just even a fraction of the old Sam back.

Today you weighed 66.4 kg! Up 4 kg from last week! Epic! The doctors consulted on your trachea today . . . we want it out!

I love you!

Sal xxx

DAY 126: SUNDAY 20 JUNE 2010

Man thrush

Hi, pumpernickle! You're so delicious and delightful, I'm really dreading going back to work. Today your mouth is awfully painful. You have oral thrush and cotton-mouth and underneath your tongue has cracked.

I feel awful for you, there's nothing worse than discomfort. You've learned to scratch which is great, but I have to shave you every day—the second-day growth seems to make you itch. I'm hanging out for you to talk. I need to hear you say you love me.

I love you.

Mwah.

Sal xxx

DAY 127: MONDAY 21 JUNE 2010

Shit day!

What can I say?! Today was definitely a shit day. A doctor gave me a five-minute-long 'talk' about the minimal prospects of a recovery and 'just how ill you are'! Just what I needed the day before I start back at work full time . . . great. All I want to do is quit now so I can look after you all day and night, but financially we just couldn't do it. It sucks and I hate it, but I really don't have any other choice but to work right now . . . I'm scared, alone and exhausted.

All I want is to have you back.

I love you.

Sal xxx

DAY 128: TUESDAY 22 JUNE 2010

Down and out

Pretty down and out today. The respiratory team told us it is now our decision to take your trachea out—all the implications fall on us—ie: if you die (a possibility) they have no liability! Are you ready for it out now? I've been listening to the music box you gave me when you were at camp in NY—it makes me feel closer to you. I'm really starting to feel lost. I need you now. I really need your voice, touch . . . everything. I want our lives to be put back together.

I'm really hurting . . . I love you.

Mwah.

Sal xxx

DAY 130: THURSDAY 24 JUNE 2010

Trachea out and speaking!

OMG! What a massive and remarkable day! I am ecstatic with joy/pride! Today they took your trachea out and to everyone's surprise, you started talking! It's all in groans, but we can make out your words. Everyone's saying you're a medical mystery and miracle! They thought it would take months and months before you would even start forming letters! You told me you loved me and I cried like a baby!

You think it's 2009—you're 22, living at home and going to uni! How funny! Well, it's a year on but I'm just happy you remember me and still love me! I asked you who I am and you said 'My fiancée, Sal.' I have been waiting to hear you say that! OMG! I am just shell-shocked with love! I feel like our life is back now! I love you!

Sal xxx

DAY 131: FRIDAY 25 JUNE 2010

Mr Romantic

Mmm, hello handsome! After I worked this morning, I sat next to you and said hello, while holding your hand. You, ever so handsome, pulled my hand to your lips, tilted your head and kissed my hand! It was so amazingly adorable—I loved it!

Your voice and talking has improved today, it's incredible to see how fast it's coming along! You keep telling me you love me, which blows me away every time, but you don't believe it's 2010 and we live together—you keep telling me I'm a liar. It's so cute. It was an epic day of falling in love all over again, I feel like you're back and our life can start all over again!

I LOVE YOU!

Sal xxx

DAY 133: SUNDAY 17 JUNE 2010

When it rains, it pours

You're probably wondering from the title of today's entry what else has gone wrong. Well, last night your dad had a mild heart attack. As if anything else could go wrong! All I need now is for your mum to collapse and we're up shit creek without a paddle or a canoe. You're slowly improving, though. You won't talk to anyone but me—except the odd 'yes', 'no' and 'TV on' to others. Your dad will be OK. He will be in hospital for approximately ten days, but the doctor told him he has to get healthy or he could have another heart attack. They said he was very, very lucky. Once again, the walls are crashing down around us, but I'll stand strong for us.

I love you more than ever.

Mwah.

Sal xxx

DAY 136: WEDNESDAY 30 JUNE 2010

Rehab

Hi, handsome! Well the rehab (brain injury) team came to assess you this morning and it wasn't the best morning. I got to you at 7.30 am, gave you a shower etc. so you looked 150 per cent presentable. You had an awful tummy ache, screaming your head off and were about to have two enemas as they walked in! They understood though—I hope. I gave them a USB with videos of your capabilities. It's still going to be a few months until you're in rehab, though. You also went in the hydrotherapy pool for the first time today. You walked a lot and it's a heated pool so I think you liked it.

It was a full-on day so you fell asleep at 4.30 pm! We had lots of hugs and kisses today . . . I love you!

Mwah.

Sal xxx

DAY 137: THURSDAY 1 JULY 2010

Miracle

Sometimes it takes a stranger to remind you how far life has come and how far we have all grown. I feel like I'm 54, not 24 years old. I feel like I've already lived my life, with all we have gone through in the last four and a half months. And then I come home to an empty house full of memories of our old life and I'm reminded just how lonely I am in all of this. It's an epic journey, one we've only just begun and we can make it through. It's winter and the bed is cold without you. The house is silent. I have zero housework (I'm never home) and I have no-one to cook for. I can't imagine another two years alone until you come home—that's how long they say it will be.

I love you.

Sal xxx

DAY 139: SATURDAY 3 JULY 2010

Angry Anderson

Well, your anger is close to being out of control. It's super-hard—we don't know why you're angry at us because you can't talk anymore so we can't help you. The recovery is all up to you, Sam. We can give you all the tools and the support in the world, but no-one, no-one can choose to take the recovery steps except you.

I can't physically make you do your speech therapy, so every day you choose not to do it—another day behind you are in recovery. I just don't know what to do at the moment, I actually feel like you don't want me there to help you at all.

I love you.

Sal xxx

DAY 144: THURSDAY 8 JULY 2010

Food, buzzer, love and golf

My beautiful soulmate . . . I'm sorry I haven't written sooner, I've been so busy at work. People don't realise or understand how little time I have. I am literally out of the house and non-stop running around from 7 am til 10 pm!

Anyway, today I fed you your first proper meal! Puréed lamb, with mashed potato, pumpkin, peas and gravy! You loved it—you wolfed it down. Your fine motor skills are improving and you're super loved-up and cuddly, which I love. I've also taught you to use the nurse-call buzzer and light switch so you spent half an hour tonight switching the light on and off. I'm just in awe of how amazing you are! Oh! I also emailed Geoff Ogilvy's manager—a signed ball would be great! Ha ha!

I love you.

Sal xxx

DAY 145: FRIDAY 9 JULY 2010

Yum, more please!

Hi, handsome . . . I love you oh so much! This morning I fed you porridge and after every mouthful you mumbled, 'Yum, more please!' It was the cutest thing. Every single day I fall more and more in love with you. When I'm at work I'm literally bursting at the seams to go and see you.

I had a thought today. Seeing as February 14 (Valentine's Day) will forever be marred as the single worst day in my entire life, I'd like to make Valentine's Day have a new memory. I'd like to marry you on Valentine's Day 2013 (if you're ready). That way it will forever mark the happiest moment of my life—beginning a new life together by marrying you.

I love you.

Sal xxx

DAY 147: SUNDAY 11 JULY 2010

Loneliness

Hi, pumpkin. Well, winter really likes to remind you of how lonely you are . . . cold beds, cold, empty house. No fiancé to warm you up, or fill the house with love and laughter. I never feel as lonely as I do at night. Even if I get home late, I'm always guaranteed hours upon hours of lying in bed alone, with absolute silence. There is no-one to protect me from intruders and certainly no-one to protect me from my own thoughts. They are always the worst. It only takes around one hour of complete loneliness for depression to set in and trust me, feeling the throes of depression is awful! The house clicks and clacks and every noise is scary . . . your mind wanders into things it shouldn't. Will you live a long life with me? Will something else happen and will you be taken away from me once again? No-one knows, but I wish we did. I wish I'd know if you'll be all right; if we will be all right, together. It's so very weird, when I'm at work, it's like it hasn't happened and then I walk into the hospital, or our house and I feel like our world is falling on top of me all over again.

It's been so very, very long since I've felt the warm, loving touch of that strong man I fell in love with. I'm falling to pieces and all I need is you, the old Sam, to hold me. I know deep down it will be many, many more months before I feel that. But even more so I know that I'll never truly feel that again. What I'll feel is the touch of another Sam, someone who has been changed for eternity, and so, a new Sam and Sal will fall in love, all over again . . .

Sal xxx

DAY 148: MONDAY 12 JULY 2010

Sym's 24th

Today is Symone's 24th birthday. I told you and you said 'Wow, she's old.' I reminded you I'm 24, but because you don't believe me that it's 2010 . . . well, it's a very difficult thing! You also don't believe me that we lived together.

I'm just glad you remember me, *fullstop*! How cute!

I love you!

Sal xxx

DAY 149: TUESDAY 13 JULY 2010

Ugh! So alone!

You would never imagine how utterly lonely it is . . . coming home to an empty house, cooking for one, washing for one . . . watching mindless boring shit on TV 'cos you can't talk to anyone, and then lying in bed for hours, all alone with your thoughts, a big empty bed, empty house.

You can hear a penny drop: the silence is deafening. Every single squeak scares me. I'm all alone and you're not here to hold me, protect me, love me. The time passes extra slowly but I only sleep six hours a night. I can't fall asleep for ages and then I wake up so very tired, but I lie in bed not wanting to go out into the big, awful world. As for work, man, I just wish I was still driving you to the train station every morning to go to work. I miss you unbelievably. It hurts.

I love you.

Sal xxx

DAY 150: WEDNESDAY 14 JULY 2010

Today marks FIVE very, very long months . . .
Nothing to say really!

DAY 154: SUNDAY 18 JULY 2010

My beloved one . . .
Hi, babe. Sorry it's been a few days since I've written, I've had a pretty rough trot. I haven't been coping well, just super-depressed, almost unable to function. I've been crying at the drop of a hat. Last night I was so exhausted (I think five months of 5–6 hours' sleep is catching up with me), I had a headache and put my head on your chest . . . you were so romantic—you stroked my head!

Antonio and Deanna got engaged yesterday. Antonio asked for my blessing. It's really tearing him up that you're not 'you' for this, he wants you at the wedding so bad. It'll be in September 2011. I'm finding it hard with our wedding being postponed and all . . .

I love you.

Sal xxx

DAY 156: TUESDAY 20 JULY 2010

Romantic kisses

Hey, hunky. I'm dreading another working week ahead of me starting tomorrow. I really loved spending *all* day *every* day with you. I honestly did. Now I feel like our time together is significantly shortened, but if we want to move to a house that suits your needs (no stairs) etc., I need to work! Today we had lots of snuggles. A very romantic day. You had your infected ears cleaned out by the ENT (Ear, Nose and Throat) and also saw the dentist, had hydrotherapy and speech therapy. It was an epic day! I also taught you to write your name. I'm trying to find things to do at night when I'm home, as I'm epically lonely . . . I can only imagine how you feel.

I love you.

Sal xxx

DAY 157: WEDNESDAY 21 JULY 2010

Sammy, I love you

Hi, possum, well I worked today and then we had a bliss-fully beautiful night together. You ate dinner sitting in a normal chair and also played beats by banging your plastered feet on the ground. It didn't take long to wear you out—unusually you fell asleep at 7 pm, normally it's more like 9–10 pm, so I also got an early night.

I wonder how many times in this book I've said I'm lonely? Well, I am! Nothing causes you to break open a bottle of wine and have a massive breakdown more than the stark, cold, quiet house every single night. But I love you and I know it's only a matter of time until you're back with me in our home.

I love you.

Sal xxx

DAY 159: FRIDAY 23 JULY 2010

Engagement, schmenmagement

Hi, sweetheart, well, I'm still unsure as to why, but I just can't be happy for others at the moment. More friends got engaged tonight. I'm not sure if it's because I haven't gotten my fairytale ending yet, or the fact my wedding dress is hanging in our bedroom . . . I don't know. Well, for five and a half months now I've been wanting a tattoo to mark this life-changing event and also to give me strength. I want these lyrics by Ben Harper on my ribcage:

> *Couldn't leave you to go to heaven,*
> *I carry you in my smile,*
> *For the first time my true reflection I see,*
> *Happy ever after in your eyes.*

It's the only thing that perfectly sums up how I have felt this past five and a half months.

I love you.

Sal xxx

DAY 162: MONDAY 26TH JULY 2010

Tragedy, Illness, Death

What a shit is 2010 . . . First off, you have eight strokes. Then your dad has a heart attack and goes into chronic heart failure. Then Alyce has a horrific car accident (is luckily unhurt) *then* an old school friend/neighbour has an awful car accident which kills his new wife (26 years old) and leaves him in a critical condition. Life is seriously too short, too unfair. All I want is you and our old life back. We are *far too young* to be dealing with all of this grief and tragedy. I'm starting to lose my positive outlook and faith in life. All it seems to have in store for us is tragedy. Where is the hope?

I love you.

Sal xxx

DAY 163: TUESDAY 27 JULY 2010

I'm so in love with you

Call me crazy but I am absolutely 150 per cent undoubtedly in love with you. Every single time I feel your touch, hear your voice (when you feel like talking) or see you, my heart flutters, as if it's realising all over again that it's connecting with its mate, soulmate, a connection and bond that can never, ever be broken, not even through death.

I just want to hold you and I am guilty of smothering you when I see you. I cover you in hugs and kisses and rarely are we not touching—always holding hands, lovingly exchanging love messages. That's the great thing about our love—you don't even have to talk, the smallest touch tells all—true love.

I love you.

Sal xxx

DAY 167: THURSDAY 29 JULY 2010

Hugs and kisses

Hi, Gorgeous, I love you so infinitely. Well, the doctors have told us they haven't treated you medically for a few weeks now, which is amazing. It means that you'll move into a rehab facility soon now. This rehab place is full and can't take you yet, so you'll go to another brain injury rehab facility as an interim until the good one can take you. I tried to teach you how to use your iPhone today. It would help if you could see better, but you weren't bad! I'm looking forward to the day you can come home—I just miss you so much around the house.

My heart aches for you.

I love you.

Sal xxx

DAY 170: SUNDAY 1 AUGUST 2010

Rehab and physio

Hi, honey. Sorry I haven't written . . . I'm working six days this week so I've been flat out. It's not easy working full-time and having your entire personal life a complete mess. Well, the doctors told me due to the sheer limit of beds in the brain injury rehab centre (I'm talking 22 beds for all Queensland and half of New South Wales) you're 'months and months and months' away from going to rehab. It's bullshit because you're ready now but the healthcare system is failing you! Your mum and I have decided to split the costs to hire private physios to work with you an extra five days a week. It's still a far cry from the intense physio you need.

I love you.

Sal xxx

DAY 171: MONDAY 2 AUGUST 2010

I'll fight for you

Well, I've been spending as much time as possible over the last ten days trying to find alternate places for you to go to rehab, even trying to hire in private specialists and exploring the possibility of relocating to Sydney to get you the best possible treatment. I'll always fight my absolute utmost to get you anything you need—we were meant for each other, and I want to help you come back. I asked you today if you feel trapped in your body and you indicated 'Yes'. Sounds stupid but just for a second I want to feel my strong Sammy hold me tight and protect me—just one second. When I search my heart, it's you I find each and every time.

I love you.

Sal xxx

DAY 173: WEDNESDAY 4 AUGUST 2010

One to say I love you and two to say it with respect

I often wonder if you understand how void and lonely life is with you as you are. I'm sure you are thinking the exact same thing . . . it doesn't matter how hard I try, leaving you every night to go home, never, ever gets easier. The smallest thing makes me cry—seeing a guy run his fingers through his lover's hair, a woman jumping into her partner's arms for a hug, or two people looking at each other lovingly.

None of these things I am sure we will ever have again, yet walking through life these things pain me and rip me apart, no matter where I go. It's everywhere. I am hoping, praying, wishing, you'll come back to me and that you're not permanently disabled, like they say.

I love you.

Sal xxx

DAY 174: THURSDAY 5 AUGUST 2010

Love, all over again!

We had the most beautiful day together today . . . all day long, you and me. I gave you an ice cream and you devoured it with a big, cheeky grin! We did lots of standing practice together—I stood you up 40 times and each time we had a standing hug and kiss. We moved our hips to emulate dancing and we yelled 'Yahoo!' at the top of our lungs which made us giggle—a lot!

I spoke to the physio about starting to do some day trips home and he thought it was a good idea! Now we need a 4WD to get you and your wheelchair out and about.

Hmm, so in love. I feel like today we fell in love all over again.

I love you!

Sal xxx

DAY 177: SUNDAY 8 AUGUST 2010

Hugs, kisses and hugkiss

Gosh, I love you! It's going to sound so silly to our kids when they read this diary in 30 years, but every single day I feel like I'm falling in love all over again. Tonight I jumped in bed with you (clothes on!) *of course*—after an eleven and a half hour work day and for the first time in almost six months we had our first proper snuggle . . . me curled up in your arms, head on your shoulder. You're finally strong enough and I feel protected from the world when you hold me like that. People take so much for granted, and it's such a shame. There is nothing more precious than being held, caressed and loved by the one person in the world your soul truly connects with.

I love you.

Sal xxx

DAY 181: THURSDAY 12 AUGUST 2010

Family meeting

Darling, gorgeous soulmate! Sorry it's been so long since I've written . . . I have been exhausted! I read one of your files today (I'm not supposed to) and they have noted 'Fiancée (Sally) at present sleep deprived and at risk'. GREAT! NOT!

We had our first family meeting with your medical team in the four and a half months today. Pretty much it's three months until you go to rehab, as they are full. On a positive note they agreed to get your eyesight tested and allow you on day leave!!! So, tomorrow I'm going to drive you to our house to see Ralph and George! Your second car trip in six months!

I LOVE YOU!

Mwah!

Sal xxx

DAY 184: SUNDAY 15 AUGUST 2010

Six months, one day

Darling, I'm so sorry I have been slack writing . . . I'm utterly exhausted! I'm actually wondering what is sleep? Why don't I have time for any? I actually washed my hair today after not even having time to do that for one and a half weeks! Gross!

Tonight you screamed and carried on for hours. I couldn't figure out what was wrong, so I gave you a pen and paper as a last resort. You wrote 'I'm hungry'! Gosh! If only I'd known that earlier. You ate two tubs of custard and your first Weetbix in six months and one day! You made me mix a strawberry thickshake into the Weetbix and feed it to you—feral! But you loved it! I'm so exhausted, wondering how much longer my body will run on autopilot for.

I love you!

Sal xxx

DAY 185: MONDAY 16 AUGUST 2010

Grandpa leg crosser

Hi, handsome! You are so adorable, you have started crossing your legs like a grandpa! Ha! It looks so funny. You scoffed dinner tonight, plus two tubs of custard, a tub of puréed apple, a strawberry milkshake and two ice creams!

At 70 kg you're still 15 kg lighter than on admission BUT you look 80 kg! Ha ha! It's all fat that you're putting on when you were all muscle before with your hot athlete's body. It'll all come back in time. You also have started writing. Today you wrote 'I have feelings' and when I asked you what they were you wrote 'I love you.' GORGEOUS! Still the same old super-romantic Sammy G!

I love you!

Sal xxx

DAY 186: TUESDAY 17 AUGUST 2010

I can push myself!

Hi soulmate! Well you had an awesome day today! You went to hydrotherapy, occupational therapy and speech therapy. In OT you got a new wheelchair which is lighter and you pushed yourself six metres in it! Yay! In speech your therapist asked you to write down three words you want to practise saying this week. You picked (with a HUGE CHEEKY smile) 'Fuck', 'Homo' and 'Golf'. Ha ha ha! The therapist wasn't impressed but I was—to me it's just a sign you're back! The doctor from the rehab centre came and said you won't go there cos they can't give you the same amount of therapy as you're getting now . . . so we keep waiting for rehab to accept you.

Mwah—I love you!

Sal xxx

DAY 188: THURSDAY 19 AUGUST 2010

Hugs!

'Sigh' . . . I just watched a video of soldiers coming home and surprising loved ones . . . I spent the entire ten minutes bawling my eyes out. That moment where the couples were running into each other's arms, hugging, kissing, embracing—I just feel like we're never going to have that emotion again . . . either that or a big part of me is still waiting for the old you to come running around the corner and love me like that. Thinking of how you were before doesn't bring me joy, it just pains me to think you'll never be that person again. I want you back so bad. I feel like this is just a shell of our life together and that the four years prior to this were a dream . . .

The old you feels like a dream.

I love you.

Sal xxx

DAY 189: FRIDAY 20 AUGUST 2010

Grandpa slippers

Hello, honey. We had a *great* day together today. We spent the entire day together (it's my day off) and you wrote a shopping list for me of things I need to buy you—

- ♥ *Grandpa slippers*
- ♥ *Iced coffee*
- ♥ *Food!!!*

So Mum and I took you out to the shops (your third trip outside the hospital) and you got all of the above plus a new pair of shorts. You are writing a lot—but barely talking, which isn't good. I can't sleep again, thinking about our future . . . I need you to *talk* and tell me it'll all be OK.

I love you,

Soulmate.

Sal xxx

DAY 191: SUNDAY 22 AUGUST 2010

Help me!

Dear handsome! I worked all day today and am slowly realising I am not Wonder Woman. Come January, I can no longer working full-time and looking after you—it's far too much to handle. Imagine how much harder it'll be when you come home if I continue to work?? Shit thing is, we need the money to pay the bills, but I'm scared if I don't slow down I'll come crashing down in a spectacular way—hospitalisation for exhaustion! I'm out of the house a minimum 6.30 am–9.30 pm, so all my household chores are done after 9.30 pm. And during that 6.30 am–9.30 pm I'm working and taking care of you, seven days a week. There is zero downtime. I'm getting fat from stress and not having any time to eat properly!

I love you.

You're my world. Mwah!

Sal xxx

DAY 194: WEDNESDAY 25 AUGUST 2010

What is coping?

Sam, tonight you moaned for two hours straight. You wouldn't settle. You kept screaming you were hungry, but you'd had so much food you vomited. At 10 pm I told you I had to go home to get some sleep. I've never, ever seen you cry so hard—it truly broke my heart. We bawled our eyes out together, both from frustration. It's now 10.54 pm and I've only just got home. I cried all the way out of the hospital and all the way home. I truly feel like I'm not your fiancé, but a mother of a newborn—the characteristics are all the same, and so is 99 per cent of your behaviour.

I realised tonight I'll never have you back and I can't stand to look at old pictures or think of memories of the old you—it hurts too much. I love you.

Sal xxx

DAY 195: THURSDAY 26 AUGUST 2010

UGH!

Hi soulmate. Today we went out to to see your parents' new house and it was really fun! Except for me trying to get your wheelchair in and out of a hatchback—NOT FUN! Ha! I'm so over my car; tomorrow I'm going to get up early and go looking for a two-door 4WD, something I can just throw your chair in. It needs to be easy for me! We don't have any money to upgrade so I'll sell my car and get a four or five-year old 4WD with around 200,000 km on it. But it's only short-term, around a year or so, so it'll do! It's now 11 pm and I've just got home, you bawled your eyes out when I had to go. It's not a normal cry. It's like a little baby and it breaks me into a million pieces to see . . .

I love you!

Sal xxx

DAY 197: SATURDAY 28 AUGUST 2010

What is sleep?

Is this magical, mysterious thing called sleep even necessary? It's now 11.30 pm and sixteen and a half hours since I left home this morning. I've only just got home. It's been eleven and a half hours since I've eaten or drunk anything and my total time for 'me' over the last 24 hours has been half an hour (shower and getting dressed). I've worked and spent an agonising night with you. Once again listening to your two-hour-long moan and drone sessions and the lovely tantrums you throw! I feel so guilty and awful saying it because I know what you're going through is a million times worse but you're acting like a five year old! With now only seven hours until I have to get up for work, let's see how much sleep I get worrying about you all night.

I love you.

Sal xxx

DAY 198: SUNDAY 29 AUGUST 2010

Blessed to be a witness

11.15 pm and I've just got home again. I had an epic work day today and was able to see you. The most *amazing* thing happened tonight! I asked you to stand up and you did just that, you just *stood up*!! It was seriously, insanely amazing! It blew my mind away! Yesterday you couldn't do it at all and today, wham! On another note, a videography company which is one of my suppliers from work, made the most beautiful offer today. They want to make a two-minute film of us—a love story. How gorgeous is that! They also said if we cover their airfares they will come to Vanuatu for the wedding—and film it for FREE! Isn't that stunning! I'm so excited! Finally our life is taking positive steps FORWARD!

I love you.

Sal xxx

DAY 205: FRIDAY 4 SEPTEMBER 2010

This is life!

Sorry I haven't written in five days—it's been awful! We just had the busiest, craziest week and I've been too tired to write. But today we went into the city and you had a facial, head, foot and hand massage! You got totally pampered, then after four months of agonising . . . you . . . WERE ACCEPTED TO REHAB!!! WOOOOO HOOOOOOO! Now you have to wait for an available bed. BUT you will only be in for three months, so you'll be home in JANUARY!

YAY! I LOVE YOU!

Mwah!

Sal xxx

DAY 212: FRIDAY 10 SEPTEMBER 2010

Wheelchair vs pram

Hi, Sammy—again, sorry I haven't written. I've been so super-exhausted and depressed. I feel like I'm epically failing at work, loving you, maintaining the house, finances, making medical decisions, looking after the dogs, staying healthy—the list goes on and on. I took you to the shops today—you chucked a screaming shit fit/tantrum in the middle of the shops . . . now can you see why I feel I am failing? People stared at us, I guess 'cos we are young. That doesn't bother me—it's when I see a couple our age with a pram. That's the family I've so desperately wanted with you and I guess now we may never have it. I should be pushing a pram, not a wheelchair.

I love you.

Sal xxx

DAY 214: SUNDAY 12 SEPTEMBER 2010

La, la, love!

How did we get here, handsome? It's SEPTEMBER already! In two days you will have been hospitalised for seven months—that's crazy. Work was shit today, I almost thought I'd get fired! I haven't done anything wrong, but because I'm there slightly less than the others, I'm an easy target for blame. I've really had to stick up for myself. Tonight was awesome. I stood two metres away from you and did all sorts of hand/body movements and you followed them, all which is *huge* considering two months ago you couldn't see anything and we thought you were blind!

You're a MIRACLE!

I love you!

Mwah!

Sal xxx

DAY 215: TUESDAY 13 SEPTEMBER 2010

Yep, I love you!

Hi, gorgeous! What an epic day—work is in full throttle being two weeks into peak wedding season. Then I rushed to you and you looked so handsome. Your new size 36 pants that I bought you fit a treat. I love you so much. I really, truly do, with all of my heart and soul.

There isn't a day go by that I don't feel eternally grateful that you're still here, even if my Sammy is gone and in his place is this one. You had your eyes tested and we were all very surprised! You have vision, despite all of the medical team and specialists initially thinking you were blind.

I can't wait to be your wife.

I love you!

Sal xxx

DAY 217: THURSDAY 16 SEPTEMBER 2010

Brain Injury Rehabilitation Unit

Hi, honey! Well, yesterday you got transferred to the Brain Injury Rehabilitation Unit—what a busy day! It's very different there, the nurses don't do much, you don't have your own TV and you have to eat in the group dining hall. You go to your therapy sessions, rather than the therapists coming to you. It's like a nursing home layout, only with rehabilitation classes—it's meant to be the best in Queensland and New South Wales and very prestigious. It took four months to get you in! It looks like a shit-hole! I am more in love with you than ever. I just want you home, to hold onto. It'll be a long time until my wish comes true.

I love you.

Sal xxx

DAY 218: FRIDAY 17 SEPTEMBER 2010

Birthday present

Hello, my gorgeous man! I loved spending 12 pm–8 pm (visiting hours) with you today. This morning I went and bought you an iPad for your birthday. It should be really good for you, a big screen and lots of helpful applications for your brain rehab. It'll take a while for you to be able to use it and we need to get your double vision sorted out, but in the long run I think it'll be great for you. The rehab unit you're in is weird . . . lots of 'mentally disabled' people, which is sad. I'd love to hear everyone's stories but no-one is willing to talk.

I love you.

Sal xxx

DAY 222: TUESDAY 21 SEPTEMBER 2010

Your birthday

Hi, handsome. Yesterday was your 24th birthday. On Sunday all of your mates came in and you had a birthday party in the courtyard of the rehab unit. Yesterday all the family came in and we did the same. I gave you an iPad, Jake and Alyce got you a portable DVD player and everyone else gave you clothes—you needed them now you've put on weight. He he. Your swallow isn't so good—it's gotten weaker and you're aspirating a lot, which isn't good. I got a 'talking to' from the social worker today about 'letting go' and 'remembering to live my life too!' Well, hello—YOU ARE MY LIFE! I couldn't imagine not spending every second with you.

I love you.

Mwah!

Sal xxx

DAY 228: SATURDAY 25 SEPTEMBER 2010

Antonio and Deanna's

Tonight was Antonio and Deanna's engagement party. It's your first real outing to a social event. It went well—you lasted half an hour before wanting to leave, but I don't blame you. Everyone was fussing over you!

You have tonsillitis.

I'm exhausted so I'm off to bed.

I love you.

Sal xxx

DAY 229: SUNDAY 26 SEPTEMBER 2010

Our love will survive

It has to. There is no other choice. Tonight I watched a show about a young man (fictional) who had just lost his wife. So many things he did, I also have done over the last seven months. So many. Like wearing your clothes to bed, or staring into pictures for hours, or glancing around our home and seeing you there. I can still see you pre 'accident' strutting on the deck while chatting on the phone. It's the mannerisms. It's when I'm caught off-guard and I see you (vision) with that big, goofy smile, crazy eyes. It sends me into instant tears, as it's something I haven't seen in so long and I am so very, very scared that I'll never see it again.

I'm so unbelievably scared you'll be like this forever. I'm terrified and I don't have you to tell me it'll be OK.

I love you.

Sal xxx

QUESTIONS . . . THAT MAY NEVER BE ANSWERED

- ♥ *Will you be OK?*
- ♥ *Will you talk again?*
- ♥ *Will you walk again?*
- ♥ *Will you function normally again?*
- ♥ *Will we get married?*

Truth is . . . I don't really need to get married any more. It's the weirdest sensation. I have you, but I am so alone. It's been seven months. I don't feel like I have that intimate lover's relationship with you, because we are unable to be intimate. I guess it's like being a widow, but visiting the body every day, praying, hoping, wishing the soul will come back. I know deep-down the soul never really comes back, so what does? I am so alone when I'm not with you, I can only imagine how you feel.

I need you.

I love you.

Sal xxx

DAY 230: MONDAY 27 SEPTEMBER 2010

I miss you, a lot

Man, I miss you a lot. Not just a little bit, but a lot. I hate seeing other couples together—it just reminds me of what we are missing and then I get flashbacks of you, your smile, your laugh, your touch. It probably sounds weird but all those things were different before the strokes. I guess intimacy also . . . I guess it'll all come back with time. I know if you were talking everything would be so different—your recovery would be faster. Somehow at seven months into all of this, I know deep down this is still only early days, still just the tip of the iceberg of recovery. I know I'll never have the old Sammy back, but I'm scared it'll be years until you're functioning normally again.

I love you.

Sal xxx

DAY 231: TUESDAY 28 SEPTEMBER 2010

Music box

Hi, handsome. Well, I've been falling asleep every night to the sound of the music box you sent me from New York four years ago. It plays 'Can you feel the love tonight?' and I honestly do when I listen to it. I see you when I listen to it.

Last night you had your first good night's sleep in two weeks—you also ate all of your dinner—yay! Now that you're on antibiotics for your tonsillitis, your swallow has improved so much. Tonight it kinda became real to me how alone I would have been if you had died—I honestly don't know what I would have done. I'm still struggling at night, it feels like I know you're there, but that you're 100 million miles away.

I love you.

Sal xxx

DAY 236: SATURDAY 2 OCTOBER 2010

Lost, a lot

Again, sorry I haven't written, Sammy. Our life is so tough. I'm in the joyous throes (sarcasm!) of depression again. It's such a vicious cycle. This whole week I've been so numb, so incredibly numb. I've had awful thoughts which are tearing me down and apart. What if you don't recover any more? Can I resign my life to being your carer for the next 60 years, no kids, no 'real' life? No-one to talk back to me, just the shell of what used to be my amazing fiancé?!? I guess this stage of grief is all about the 'what ifs?'. Why us? All I ever think about is what I am going through; it must be 100 million times worse/harder for you.

I love you.

Sal xxx

DAY 237: SUNDAY 3 OCTOBER 2010

Soul destroying

No-one, except us, understands how incredibly soul-destroying this experience is. I'm so unbelievably scared that you'll never recover. I miss your voice, your warm touch, your ego, your swagger—your everything! Tonight I asked you if you could buy anything in the world, what would you buy? In your very muffled, hard-to-understand voice you said 'A new body.' That really broke me. It's like you're stuck inside and your body is failing you. I'm so scared, Sam. I'm scared you're not able to comprehend what's happened and the urgency to recover. I can't cope if you don't recover—it's so lonely and the silence is deafening without conversation.

I need my man back.

I love you.

Sal xxx

DAY 238: MONDAY 4 OCTOBER 2010

Love of my life

You're my best friend. I still can't imagine life without you. Another patient's wife let me read a book she had made about their journey so far. It's amazing. They are so lucky, though—his speech returned so quickly. Tonight I really noticed such a big physical improvement—I'm well impressed. The speech for me is still the missing link, but you're trying so hard. You gave me a great 'Hey hon' when I arrived after work today, and as always a giant smile and endless hugs. No matter how hard it gets, life with you is always like breathing easy.

I love you, soulmate.

Sal xxx

DAY 239: TUESDAY 5 OCTOBER 2010

Mr Grumpy-pants!

Hi, gorgeous. I feel awful for you today—your swallow is so weak and you aspirated so badly at lunch they have made you nil by mouth, which means they can only put liquid food in your tummy via the 'PEG' which also means you screamed *all day* and *all night*! I know you're hungry but it isn't adult behaviour—it's more like a child. It really breaks my heart to see you like that. Also, next week I'm trading in the mighty hatchback for a 4WD—it meets all our needs. You're my hero and I love you.

Mwah!

Sal xxx

DAY 240: THURSDAY 7 OCTOBER 2010

You are amazing!

Hi, handsome. We had such a wonderful day together today (my day off). You were as happy as Larry all day, your swallow has improved and you ate your entire lunch, arvo tea, dinner and supper! You're now 84.6 kg and wear a size 38 pants!

Pre-admission you were 84 kg, all muscle and a size 30–32 pants! You were super-fit and athletic—it will all come back. I felt like a teenager today—falling in love all over again. I even jumped into bed with you to have a snuggle. Did I tell you that you're my hero? You truly are invincible, invictus.

I love you.

Mwah!

Sal xxx

DAY 241: FRIDAY 8 OCTOBER 2010

Our souls truly connect

Dear soulmate, sometimes I forget to write in here and express how truly, deeply I love you. Our love is something few people are ever lucky enough to experience. I keep thinking back to the psychic who said we meet together in every life, past and present, but are always torn apart far too early, too quickly. I believe her. In all the universe,

I know, our souls truly connect. It takes one to say 'I love you' and two to say it with respect. I still read that poem you wrote me all that time ago, every day. I can still hear you reading it to me with your husky voice.

I love you.

Marry me.

Sal xxx

DAY 243: SUNDAY 10 OCTOBER 2010

You are precious

Good news, hon! Today we sold the hatchback to a young girl about 19! So finally we can buy a 4WD this week to fit your wheelchair into—woo hooo! I am so excited! On another note, Alyce and Jake bought me a one-hour massage, one-hour facial and one-hour spa treatment voucher and gave it to me, from you. Was super-sweet, they even wrote on it from you! Also, today is the first day in 243 days that I have felt like it's 'OK' for me to laugh and feel happy. Every other day before today I have always felt so sad, depressed . . . guilty when I had the 'happy' emotion.

I love you.

Mwah!

Sal xxx

DAY 245: TUESDAY 12 OCTOBER 2010

Loneliness

I'm starting to wonder how often I can write about being lonely . . . but that's what life is . . . lonesome. I realised tonight for the first time that we both need to deal with profound loss. You for your abilities, me for my partner. It's like my heart is made of glass and was shattered on the day it all happened . . . that you suffered your strokes. My heart is broken and irreparable. I'm lost without you. Our house is full of memories of you . . . pacing on the phone on the deck, making pizzas, showering. I can still see you there and it hurts so much. I love you so much, Sam, I truly do.

We had a family meeting today with the entire medical team. They say you are making 'significant' gains.

I love you.

Sal xxx

DAY 249: SATURDAY 16 OCTOBER 2010

Ugh! Fuck you responsibility!

Hi, handsome! I got up at 6 am today, worked 8 am–7 pm, went and saw you, then went to Sam and Alex's engagement/ going away party, and just got home at 12.45 am! Talk about busy. Was such an exhausting party. Everyone asks me about you 24/7, which is really sweet but everyone wants to sit and tell me what a great job I am doing, ask me how I cope etc. etc. I'd love to just *not* talk sometimes! It's like, hello! I live this 24/7, seven days a week, the last thing I wanna do after an 11-hour day is talk about how shit life is. Sorry, Sammy, for the rant.

I love you.

Sal xxx

DAY 259: TUESDAY 26 OCTOBER 2010

Sorry I haven't written

I just can't

I'm not coping

I tested 'very high' for Major Depression . . . ugh!

Sorry. I love you.

Sal xxx

DAY 265: MONDAY 1 NOVEMBER 2010

Tatters

Handsome. I am so sorry I haven't written . . . I just haven't been coping and it's been super-busy. I just want our life back, you back. I miss you, but I've been so numb, so very, very numb. It's like I'm on auto and I can't feel anything.

All the memories of our old life are disappearing at the speed of light and I just can't seem to hold onto any of them, or the feelings of how you used to make me feel. It's just numbness. It's like the old you, the old us never existed and now we are just this . . . Stuck. A patient/carer relationship. I want a partner, a lover, a best friend back and I'm so scared I'll never get it. I need you.

I love you.

Sal xxx

DAY 267: THURSDAY 4 NOVEMBER 2010

No full moon

Hi, gorgeous! It's not even a full moon and I am wired! I've vacuumed past 11.30 pm so I don't think the neighbours will be happy! Tomorrow is a big day . . . Quest Newspapers are coming to take a picture of us for a story they are writing about our survival post-stroke.

We had a great day today. I cut your hair, we had long afternoon cuddles and watched 'The Simpson's' movie. You walked to dinner and bed, which is huge, and your stride is really improving. As usual I miss having you at home.

I love you.

Sal xxx

DAY 269: SATURDAY 6 NOVEMBER 2010

You are a superstar!

What an epic day! The florist for one of my weddings didn't turn up so I had to make a bouquet and 10 centrepieces literally out of scraps of flowers left over from another wedding! BUT YOU . . . you blew my mind tonight! I accidentally let go of you when I was helping you walk, and you took six massive steps on your own! You just went for it! Then you lost your balance and I supported you again, but more importantly you took your first steps in eight months and three weeks! Isn't that amazing! And to think they told me you'd never walk again! Ha! You are INVICTUS!

I love you!

Sal xxx

DAY 271: TUESDAY 9 NOVEMBER 2010

NOTE: You are my eternal soulmate!

It'll sound silly but I cried for hours tonight. A character on a TV show died and her husband was left grieving. It was so unbelievably realistic in its portrayal. Minor details, like him smelling and holding her wallet, I do that. Remembering her walk around the house, I do that. Sitting for hours, wardrobe open, staring at her clothes, unable to move, I do that. It really broke me down and made me realise that even after almost nine months, grieving never ends. Even though you're still here, it's a grief for a loss of life, our life and all that was.

Now, to open a new door and start a new day with all that was lost but one thing . . . our love.

I love you.

Sal xxx

DAY 277: MONDAY 15 NOVEMBER 2010

Baby steps

Mmm, hello amazingly wonderful, incredibly inspiring fiancé! This has been such a busy yet stunning week . . . you have walked up to fifty metres on your own with me only tapping you gently every so often to guide you in the right direction! You are walking 80 per cent on your tiptoes but it's still amazing! I am so incredibly awe inspired and proud. The look on your face is priceless when you realise what you're doing! And finally you're settling at night and chilling out watching movies rather than needing me to sit with you at all hours of the night! YAY! So positives on all sides!

I love you so, so, so, so, so much!

Mwah!

Sal xxx

DAY 292: MONDAY 29 NOVEMBER 2010

The media

Hi, precious! Well life is honestly just a million miles an hour and I'm too busy to write every day. The last two weeks have been epic. Our love story has been featured in the *North-West News* and *Courier-Mail*! You are progressing in leaps and bounds and your sense of humour is returning! You're still always hungry, though! I'm loving you more than ever.

I love you.

Sal xxx

DAY 298: SUNDAY 5 DECEMBER 2010

L.O.V.E.

I wish I wrote more often. It's like I'm half asleep 24/7 trying to do a million things at once . . . never-ending exhaustion. Well, this weekend will be awesome. The one and only GEOFF OGILVY has invited you to meet him at the Coolum PGA! I'm taking you for two days so it'll be an awesome little pre-Christmas getaway. Your speech is still well . . . only a few words are said and aren't very clear. You're still walking but as always, on your tiptoes so very unbalanced and I'm super in love with you!

I just vacuumed and it's almost midnight . . . but it's the ONLY time I have to do it!

Mwah, mwah, mwah! I love you!

Sal xxx

DAY 350: TUESDAY 4 JANUARY 2011

A shooting star once told me . . .

Wow, it really has been a long time since I wrote! You came home over Christmas so I didn't really get a chance to write.

For you, every day is a struggle. You've written down for me your number one goal for 2011—'to talk'. That really is the hardest part for everyone, it's the missing link. You're now writing in full sentences, which I think is amazing! To me it shows growth in both your fine motor skills and cognitive thinking.

Food is still a major issue. You actually moan out loud (very frickin' loud) virtually 24/7 for food and when you can't have it you actually work yourself up so much you hyperventilate and actually throw a tantrum. Yep . . . that's the only way to describe it!

Over Christmas I got to take you home for two weeks, which was great! Exhausting (as you need me to take you to the loo every single hour on the hour *all* night) but still amazing. Ninety-eight per cent of the time you're this all-consuming, self-obsessed person and 2 per cent of the time my Sammy emerges and life is bliss. It is so very hard to pull someone out from that sheer depth of . . . I don't know what to call it. It's exhausting. You actually are so physically and mentally draining on others as you need stimulation almost every minute! No word of a lie. You are that demanding you require 24-hour care. We are halfway now; I believe, it will take another ten months to get the speech going and those heels on the ground. It feels like no improvement is occurring, when it actually is, just in super-slow time.

I'm still madly in love with you. I just wish we had more time together when the real Sammy G can be glimpsed there on those 2 per cent of occasions.

I love you.

Sal xxx

DAY 360: THURSDAY 6 JANUARY 2011

Memories

I'm going to admit the most terrifying thing of all . . . almost a year on, and all the memories have started to fade away of our old life. Sometimes I find myself searching my brain for glimpses of how it used to feel, your old smell, touch . . . and it's scary how immersed we are now in this world that all those memories are fading away. I'm so very scared I'll lose them forever. It's so far on now and I've lived alone longer than I lived with you, it's almost like you never lived here at all and that terrifies me. I feel starkly cold and emotionless, unattached to life, and it scares me so much. When will the real Sammy G come back to me?

I love you.

Sal xxx

DAY 386: TUESDAY 1 FEBRUARY 2011

Sammy soulmate

I'm going to guess that if you're reading this you have noticed I am suffering from depression. The highs and lows in this diary make it obvious, I guess . . . I super, super love you. Over the last week you have really calmed down in terms of your behaviour. It's like a small light has switched on. It looks like you'll be coming 'home' in April now. We will rent out our three-storey townhouse—it isn't wheelchair suitable. We are meant to be moving in with your parents. I am also looking at places to rent. It's stressful. I'll be taking 3+ months off work and then slowly going back. I need my sanity. You still need 24/7 care. Literally 24/7.

I love you.

Sal xxx

DAY 390: MONDAY 5 FEBRUARY 2011

LOVE

Sam, I really miss you. I see you every day but the old Sam, I miss so much. I'm losing the memories of our old life and it's really scary. I don't know *if* or *when* you'll ever come back. I need you.

I love you.

I miss you.

Ever thine,

ever mine,

ever ours.

Sal xxx

DAY 401: WEDNESDAY 16 FEBRUARY 2011

Wowsa—I love you!

Hi, gorgeous. Well, the one-year mark has now passed since your strokes, it was hard. Three o'clock on 14 February 2011 marked the year, also . . . Valentine's Day. You are so gorgeous, you gave me a dozen red roses. I don't think you really understood the day, but your mental clarity is really picking up. Today for the very first time, you wrote 'Sal, how are you coping?' It blew my mind away.

On Monday you asked (written) . . . 'Was it my fault?' That broke my heart. I've told you many times what happened, but you forget. You know you had suffered a brain injury even before I told you you had had a stroke.

My heart aches for you.

I love you.

Sal xxx

DAY 429: THURSDAY 24 MARCH 2011

Totally lost in love

Oh Sammy. I just need something to get me through. I'm so lost, so in love. I miss you so much. I hate our situation but I hate coming home every night without you. You'll be discharged soon, and I'm starting to pack. We're moving in with your parents. I want you back so bad, but I feel you're lost in this . . . this . . . inner world, inside your brain. I feel I'm losing control over it all, and *all* I want is you. I'd die a million times over in the most horrific way just to get you back.

I need you.

I love you.

Sal xxx

DAY 432: SUNDAY 27 MARCH 2011

Moving

Never in a million years did I think it'd be this hard to pack . . . strangely it's been too easy and then bam! I'm sitting on the kitchen bench wrapping glasses and I'm flooded with a memory from the day we moved in. It was a Tuesday, 30 September 2009. I can see you sitting on the floor of the lounge, putting everything together.

Our first home, the beginning of our lives . . . all here, in boxes. This was meant to be our marital home and instead only after five months here, you never came home. I've been living alone for nine and a half months, almost fourteen months after your strokes. Epic sadness. I wish I could have brought you home.

I love you.

Sal xxx

A NEW LIFE
TALK, TALK, TALK
'STILNOX'
XXX

DAY 448: SATURDAY 14 MAY 2011
(15 MONTHS)

Discharge and Stilnox

Sammy soulmate. Wow. On Friday 13 May 2011 you were officially discharged from hospital! Almost fifteen months to the day of your strokes. It feels amazing to have brought you home, and now we live with your parents. On Wednesday 11 May we gave you your first ever dose of Stilnox, after six months of trying to get a doctor to prescribe it. It's a sleeping tablet, but for some reason it brings you to a higher level of consciousness—AND YOU TALK NORMALLY! Just proves you're not brain damaged!

I love you.

Sal xxx

DAY 484: MONDAY 6 JUNE 2011

Sammy my miracle

Sam, it's been three weeks since your discharge from hospital. It feels so incredibly amazing to have you home. We are so lucky to have one another, and I feel blessed every minute I am able to share with you. I cannot imagine how life could have been without you, as survival was and is always the only choice. Look how far we have come! It is amazing. Every day you work harder, and every day you get a little bit better. I am so proud of you and everything you do. I cannot wait to spend eternity in your arms.

Love always.

Sal xxxx

DAY 487: THURSDAY 9 JUNE 2011

Sixteen months on

Sammy, It's now sixteen months since your strokes. I am so proud of you and how far you have come. Sixteen months ago I saw you almost die, claw your way back from the brink of death and now blossom into such an extraordinary man. You are exactly the man I always imagined you would be. It will be an amazing future together; just as the last five years have been so far. Our life can only get better from here.

I love you.

Sal xxx

Epilogue

Sam and Sally plan to spend every Valentine's Day together re-making what happened on that fateful day in 2010. So, on 14 February 2013, they plan to get married on a peaceful beach surrounded by those who have supported them through their journey, with the vows:

Ever thine,
ever mine,
ever ours

Glossary

Arginine an amino acid used as a dietary supplement

Blood stealer a port inserted into a blood vessel to drain blood from the body for medical testing

BP the pressure exerted by circulating blood against the blood vessel walls, and a main indicator of vital signs

Boulis a way of quickly injecting matter into the body in a large amount, rather than a large amount over a long period of time

BPM breaths per minute: a key indicator of a person's respiratory rate

Brain tap or EVD external ventricular drain: a device used to drain excess fluid off the brain that is causing inter-cranial pressure

CPAP Continuous Positive Airway Pressure: a mode of respiratory ventilation

ECG a monitor to measure the electrical activity of the brain

ENT ear, nose and throat

Fentanyl a potent painkiller

Glasgow Coma Scale a neuro-logical scale used to identify a person's conscious state

Heart line a catheter passed through a vein to monitor the heart

ICP intercranial pressure: the pressure within the skull that keeps the brain safe from harm and which can in turn

SALLY NIELSEN

build up and cause brain
damage

Leg pressuriser   a mechanically
inflated device used to
increase blood flow in the
limbs

MRI   Magnetic Resonance
Imaging: a medical imaging
technique used to visualise
internal structures of the
body

Midazalom   a short-acting drug
used to sedate a person

MCS   minimally conscious
state: the state in which a
person is not in a persistent
vegetative state, yet is not
awake and aware of their
surroundings

PDO   a congenital hole in the
heart which does not gener-
ally affect a person's
day-to-day health

Pneumonia   an infection of the
lungs

Pneumothorax   the presence of
air or gas in the lung cavity

Propofol   a short-acting drug
used to maintain anaesthesia

Pseudomona   a bacteria that
can cause infection

PVS   persistent vegetative state

Sputum   mucus that builds up
in the lower airways and
causes obstruction

Subarachnoid haemorrhage
bleeding into the area
surrounding the brain

Suctioning   a technique used to
drain the chest of a build-up
of fluids, using a thin, long
tube placed down the trachea,
sucking the fluid back up

Tobramyson   an antibiotic used
to treat bacterial infections

Tracheotomy   a medical proce-
dure used to insert a
breathing tube into the throat

TPC   a high-flow ventilator
which allows the patient to be
weaned off mechanical ventilation by providing a limited
amount of air flowing into
the trachea

VRE   Vancomyson-resistant
Enterococcus: a dangerous
hospital super-bug which is
resistant to antibiotics